UPAMĀNA
IN
INDIAN PHILOSOPHY

UPAMĀNA IN INDIAN PHILOSOPHY

Dr. S.K. BELVAKAR PRIZE BOOK
Approved by
THE UNIVERSITY OF POONA

Late **Dr. SHIV KUMAR**
Centre of Advanced Study in Sanskrit,
University of Poona

EASTERN BOOK LINKERS
DELHI INDIA

Published by :
EASTERN BOOK LINKERS
5825, New Chandrawal Road, Jawahar Nagar,
Delhi-110007

ISBN :-81-85133-79-4

Second Revised Edition, 1994

Price Rs. 400-

Typesetting by :
Amar Printing Press
8/25, Vijay Nagar, Delhi-9
Phone : 7252362

To

The Revered Memory of

Late Doctor (MISS) CHITRAREKHA V. KHER, Poona,

With Love and Gratitude

INTODUCTION

Upamāna is an independent means of knowledge in the systems of Nyāya, Pūrvamīmāṁsā and the Advaita school of Uttaramīmāṁsā. While going through the details of Upamāna in the texts we find that the conceptions of different schools or of the same school in different works do not absolutely coincide. For example, in the system of Nyāya we come across divergence of opinion regarding the instrumentality in Upamāna. Gautama equates it with the well known similarity, Vātsyāyana takes it as the statement of a reliable person conveying similarity, whereas Uddyotakara thinks it as the knowledge of the well known similarity. These views lead to the further divergence in their theories of the psychological process in Upamāna. Thus, the development of the concept of Upamāna even in a single system needs a comprehensive review.

The upholders of Upamāna as an independent means of knowledge also differ in details. For example, there is the divergence of opinion regarding the nature of resultant knowledge through Upamāna. The Pūrvamīmāṁsakas and the Advaita Vedāntins are on one side and the Naiyāyikas on the other. According to the Pūrvamīmāṁsakas the resultant knowledge pertains to the similarity which the remembered object bears to the directly perceived one. But, according to the Naiyāyikas it is the knowledge that a certain word denotes a certain class of objects. Thus the comparative study of the concept of Upamāna is still a desideratum.

Similarly, the other systems agree in rejecting Upamåna as an independent means of cognition. Their grounds for doing so, however, are very different. Some include it under inference, osme under verbal testimony, some under perception while some others include it under remembrance. These scattered views, however, deserve a systematic study. Agian, the divergence of opinion presents further problems regarding validity of the grounds for the inclusion of Upamāna in some means of knowledge or other. We, further, face the question regarding the place of Upamāna in the valid or non-valid means of knowledge. These problems require a detailed consideration.

Here we propose to study the problems regarding Upamāna in the context of Nyāya, Pūrvamīmāṁsā and Advaita Vedānta in particular and of the other systems of Indian philosophy in general. In course of discussion an attempt is made to co-ordinate and evaluate the answers supplied by various systematists to the problems regarding the nature, kind and process involved in Upamāna.

As the literature of each of the systems is very vast, it has compelled us to limit the study to the selected works of each of the systems. As regards the selection of the sources, the texts which are of basic importance and have constructive value are selected for the present study. We have selected as far as possible the sūtras, the bhāṣyas, and the vārttikas as well as some celebrated works of each system. The selection of these texts is prompted by the consideration that the sūtras represent the seeds of the thought, the bhāṣyas and the vārttikas indicate their development into a discipline in the form of concrete and possible criticism and the celebrated works offer a picture of a fullfledged system. The celebrated works of different systems consulted here are the manuals which contain the elaboration or compendium of what has been said in original texts of the system. It has been our aim to settle the chronological controversies. The latest accepted views regarding the age of the texts is generally followed. The works of modern scholars are also consulted for a clearer and critical presentation of the subject matter.

References to the concept of Upamāna occur partly in the works dealing with perticular systems such as the *Nyāya theory of knowledge, Epistemology of Bhāṭṭa school of Pūrvamīmāṁsā, Six ways of knowledge,* etc., or in the standard works dealing with the history of Indian Philosophy. The problem however, is not studied independently and systematically. The present work is therefore, devoted mainly to what has been written by the ancient *ācāryas* in the original texts of different systems. In such cases, the author cannot claim much originality in the real sense of the term. But still, it is hoped that the work will fulfil a hitherto unsatisfied need of providing systematically an account of the views of the authors of different schools regarding various problems about Upamāna on the basis of the original Sanskrit texts of different systems. It has given some scope for the author to exhibit critical attitude and independent judgement wherever necessary.

The controversies cover a wide range of problems. therefore, a definite arrangement is followed in the discussion. The material presented is systemwise and topicwise. The views of the upholders of Upamāna as an independent means of knowledge are discussed first and the discussion is followed by the views of the critics of Upamāna. The chronological order is always kept in view so as to throw light on the development of the grounds of either side. It is realised that in such cases the parctice of dealing with the views of the authors of particular period at one place cannot be followed. Thruogh it is a good plan in itself, yet it would be ill-adapted for the present study. We have studied the problem of Upamāna with a view to trace the development of throught in a single system also so as to determine the contribution of a particular author of a system to the problem. Besides, the discussion could not have been more appropriately and effectively presented under any other arrangement.

In course of discussion usually adopted English renderings of Sanskrit technical terms have been accepted and the original term is given in brackets to avoid confusion. We had to depart form the usual translation sometimes to make the meaning as literal as possible. However, when we found no translation which can retain the original shade of meaning, we preferred to retain the original Sanskrit term only. For example, we have retained the original Sanskrit term Upamāna, for the generally accepted translations like analogy or comparison do not fully represent the shade of meaning conveyed by the Naiyāyikas and the through it. The meaning given by the Naiyāyikas and the Mīmāṁsakas is more comprehensive than that conveyed by translations.

At the end of discussion we have given a list of works consulted during the preparation of the work. In most of the cases, the important passages have been quoted in original in the footnotes. In some cases, to avoid elaboration, only the reference to the original text is given in the footnote when the original passage is quoted in some other footnote or when it is not considered to be necessary.

I take this opportunity to express thanks to all those who helped me in my present venture. I undertook the present work with my submitting of a monograph to the University of Poona. I was encouraged in my work by the award of Dr. S. K. Belvalkar Prize by the University. I am deeply grateful to Dr. S. D. Joshi, Director, Centre of

Advanced Study in Sanskrit, who pursuaded me to undertake the present study. I am also grateful to Professor Dr. S. S. Barlingay, Department of Philosophy, University of Poona, for many valuable suggestions. My thanks are also due to my friend Dr. Mohan Chand for his help especially in getting this book published. I am thankful to shri Sham Lal, proprietor, Eastern Book Linkers, Delhi-7, who extended to me a more than usual professinal cooperation.

ABBREVIATIONS

A.S.	Aṣṭasāhasrī
B.T.B.	Bauddha Tarkabhāṣā
G.	Gauḍapādabhāṣya on S.K.
Jay.	Jaytīrtha
J.M.	Jayamaṅgalā
Kir.	Kiraṇāvalī
M.M.	Mānameyodaya
M.V.	Māṭharavṛtti
N.A.V.	Nyāyāvatāravārttikavṛtti
N.B.	Nyāyabhāṣya
N.B.T.	Nyāyabinduṭīkā
N.C.	Nyāyacandrikā
N.D.M.	Nayadyumaṇiḥ
N.K.	Nyāyakandalī
N.Ku.	Nyāyakusumāñjalī
N.M.	Nyāyamañjarī
N.P.	Nyāyapariśuddhi
N.R.	Nyāyaratnākara
N.S.	Nyāyasūtra
N.Sāra	Nyāyasāra
N.Sa.S.	Nyāyasārasaṁgraha
N.S.M.	Nyāyasiddhāntamañjarī
N.V.	Nyāyavārttika
N.V.T.T.	Nyāyavārttikatātparyaṭīkā
P.B.	Praśastapādabhāṣya

P.K.M.	Prameyakamalamārtaṇḍa
P.N.T.	Pramāṇanayatattvāloka
P.P.	Prakaraṇapañcikā
P.Pad.	Pramāṇapaddhati
P.P.G.V.	Parapakṣagirivajra
P.Pra.	Pramāṇaprakaraṇa
P.R.K.	Prasthānaratnākara
P.V.	Pramāṇavārttika
S.B.	Śābarbhāṣya
S.C.	Sāṁkhyacandrikā
S.D.	Śāstradīdpikā
S.K.	Sāṁkhyakārikā
S.K.	Sāṁkhyakārikā
S.T.K.	Sāṁkhyatattvakaumudī
S.P.B.	Sāṁkhyapravacanadhāṣya
S.V.	Ślokavārttika
Tarkas.	Tarkasaṁgraha
T.B.	Tarkabhāṣā (Jaina)
T.R.	Tārkikarakṣā
T.S.	Tattvasaṁgraha
T.S.P.	Tattvasaṁgrahapañcikā
V.P.	Vedāntaparibhāṣā
Y.D.	Yuktidīpikā
Y.M.D.	Yatīndramatadīpikā
Y.S.	Yogasūtra

CONTENTS

INTRODUCTION		ix
ABBREVIATIONS		xiii
CHAPTERS		
1.	Pramā and Pramāṇa	1
2.	Nyāya concept of Upamāna	13
3.	Pūrvamīmāṁsā concept of Upamāna	63
4.	Advaita Vedānta concept of Upamāna	98
5.	Bhāsarvajña on Upamāna	111
6.	Vaiśeṣika concept of Upamāna	114
7.	Sāṁkhya concept of Upamāna	119
8.	Buddhist concept of Upamāna	123
9.	Jaina concept of Upamāna	129
10.	Viśiṣṭādvaita Vedānta concept of Upamāna	132
11.	Dvaita Vedānta concept of Upamāna	137
12.	Śuddhādvaita Vedānta concept of Upamāna	142
13.	Dvaitādvaita Vedānta concept of Upamāṇa	145
14.	Resumé	147
SELECTED BIBLIOGRAPHY		160
INDEX		163

CHAPTER I

Pramā And Parmāṇa

Knowledge in the arena of Indian philosophy developed as an aid to metaphysics. It provides the method for the proper understading of the metaphysical investigations regarding the nature of the ultimate reality and relation between the ultimate reality and the empirical self as well as the objective world. Though every system of Indian philosophy devotes a considerable part of discussion to the epistemological and logical problems, yet their chief aim was to provide methodological explanation for metaphysical investigation. The sages who expound differnt systems of philosophy realised the nature of ultimate reality through yogic practices. They tried to convey their supernatural and mystic experiences through words of various āgamas precisely and methodologically. Epistemology was sought as a method for correct understanding of the metaphysical experiences handed down to us. As a result, unlike Western philosophy 'logic' could not develop as a branch of study independent of metaphysical colouring in the arena of Indian Philosophy. The study of epistemological and logical problems in Indian philosophy under the heading 'nyāya' which aims at discussing the process of knowing and argumentation cannot be called logic in the strict sense of the term. Logic in west is understood as formal form of argumentation but the Indian philosophy does not demarcate formal from informal argumentation and consequently does not differentiate logic from means of knowledge. Moreover, the scope of nyāya is wider than that of logic. The former deals with all the means of knowledge with a metaphysical colouring whereas 'logic' is peimarily concerned with Inferential problems. Thus, 'nyāya' is the study of the means of knowing and the means of testing this knowledge and does not restrict its scope only to the formal logic.

In the works on various systems of Indian philosophy we come across minute details of various problems regarding epistemology. It is true that the discussion is the result of the extension of metaphysical problems. But still, it is also not wrong that the importance of the epistemological problems is never underestimated in the systems of Indian philosophy. It is admitted on all hands that the true knowledge of the objects is the source and the indispensable means of the attainment of the highest end of life, liberation or *mokṣa*. Since the means of knowledge provide the path for correct understanding of the worldly objects as well as metaphysical investigations, the problems of knowledge find an important place in the systems of Indian philosophy.

Before taking up the problems of Upamāna proper it will be worthwhile to discuss in brief theories of different schools of Indian philosophy regarding the valid knowledge (*pramā*) and the means of vaild knowledge (*pramāṇa*).

Knowledge, in the context of philosophical investigations, may be roughly called convictions regarding reality and the means of knowledge the methods of explaining them. These convictions in general may be brought under the broad heading of *jñāna* which denotes all kinds of knowledge, true or false. When, however, man comes across various convictions regarding the same thing, he feels to varify their validity through various methods which may be roughly termed as pramāṇas. Perhaps, with this intention Vātsyāyana states that Nyāya means the examination of an object through the pramāṇas.[1] The basic aim of the pramāṇas is to test the vailidity of various convictions. But, the convictions which stand the test of validity are the *pramā* which denotes true or valid knowledge. Thus, *pramāṇa* in Indian philosophy has twofold purpose of testing the validity of conviction and to give to rise to new vaild convictions.

It is admitted on all hands that *pramā* is the true or valid knowledge. However, it begs the question regarding the test or the peculiar characteristic of validity itself. In other words, what is the factor which makes a conviction valid ? This gives rise to the divergence of views regarding the mark or the truth of valid knowledge and consequently the definition of *pramā* itself.

According to the Buddhas the truth of knowledge consists in its practical value. They define *pramā* as the knowledge which reveals an object that is capable of successful volition,[2] or as the knowledge which makes us reach the object revealed by it.[3] Kamalaśīla, however, further clarifies that the valid knowledge refers to a possible successful action; though not to the actual achievement of the object.[4] In all these cases, it is common that the validity of knowledge depends upon the success in the practical activity.

According to the Naiyāyikas, the validity of knowledge consists in the objectivity or the faithfulness of the knowledge to the object. The *parmā* is generally defined by the Naiyāyikas as the knowledge which informs of the existence of something in a place where it actually exists. Or, in other words, *pramā* is the knowledge which predicates of something a property really possessed by it.[5] The Prabhākara school of Pūrvamīmāṁsā[6] and the Dvaita,[7] the Dvaitādvaita[8] and the Śuddhādvaita[9] schools of Uttaramīmāṁsā also accept conformity of knowledge to the object as a mark of valid knowledge.

The Viśiṣṭādvaita school of Uttaramīmāṁsā holds that the validity of knowledge consists in both the faithfulness to the object and prompting to the fruitful activity. The valid knowledge is defined there as that which apprehends an object as it really exists and which prompts fruitful activity.[10]

According to the Advaita school of Uttaramīmāṁsā, the validity of knowledge consists in non-contradictoriness. The followers of this school define *pramā* as the uncontradicted knowledge of an object.[11] They do not accept novelty as an essential factor for valid knowledge. Nor do they oppose the view of considering novelty as a mark of valid knolwedge. That is why Dharmarāja Adhvaryu offers two definitions of *pramā* with and without novelty as a mark of *pramā*.[12]

The Bhāṭṭa school of the Pūrvamīmāṁsā considers the correspondence to the object, novelty and non-contradictoriness as the test of validity. Pārthasārathi Miśra defines valid knowledge as the knowledge which represents the real nature of an object, which was not attained earlier and which is not contradicted by a sublating knowledge.[13]

The Sāṁkhyas hold that the validity of knowledge consists in certainty (undoubtedness), correspondence to the object and novelty as marks of the validity of knowledge. Vācaspati Miśra defines *pramā* as the *cittavṛtti* (modification of *citta*) which apprehends an object that is undoubted, real and unknown.[14]

The Vaiśeṣikas consider certainty (lack of doubt), non-contradictoriness and definiteness as the marks of valid knowledge. Praśastapāda divides knowledge into *vidyā* and *avidyā*[15] which correspond to the pramā (valid knowledge) and *pramā* (non-valid knowledge) respectively. Śrīdhara defines *vidyā* as firm, uncontradicted and definite cognition.[16] Thus, the definition introduces definiteness (*adhyavasāya*) as a mark of valid knowledge.

According to the Jaina logicians definiteness is the essentail mark of valid knowledge. Vādidevasūri defines valid means of knowledge as a definite knowledge which reveals itself and the other objects.[17] The characteristic of definiteness here, however, does not differ essentially from the view of the Naiyāyikas because definiteness is further stated by Jaina logicians themselves to be the determination of an object in the from in which it really exists.[18] Siddhasena considers non-contradictoriness in place of definiteness as a mark of *pramā*.[19] The definition of *pramāṇa* offered by Akalaṅka[20] reveals that he considers non-contradictoriness and novelty as the marks of valid knowledge.

Thus all the systemetists unanimously hold validity or truth as the characteristic of *pramā* but differ in respect of the mark of validity or truth. The above discussion of the nature of *pramā* further reveals that according to some schools like the Sāṁkhya and the Pūrvamīmāṁsā novelty also is an essential part or diffentia of valid knowledge. Some systematists like the Vaiśeṣikas and the Jainas do not consider novelty as a mark of valid knowledge since they include remembrance (*smṛti*) into the case of valid knowledge. Some schools like the Advaita are indifferent to the controversy. Dhramarāja Adhvaryu defines *pramā* in two ways with and without validity as the mark of valid knowledge. Here, the crux of the problem lies in the acceptance or rejection of validity of remembrance as a means of knowledge. The Mīmāṁsakas and the Sāṁkhyas have accepted novelty as a mark of *pramā* to exclude remembrance from the domain of valid knowledge. The Jainas also accept remembrance among the forms of valid mediate knowledge. The Advaita Vedānta is indifferent to the problem. The Naiyāyikas consider the peresentative knowledge (*anubhūti*) as a mark of *pramā* and exclude remembrance which is not the presentation of an object but a reproduction of previous experience solely caused by the impressions of past experience. The recognition of novelty as an essential factor of valid knowledge further poses the question of the ground for inclusion of the persistent knowledge of the same object (*dhārāvāhika jñāna*) into the valid knowledge because the persistent knowledge is considerd as a form of valid knowledge by all systematists. The different schools assign different reasons to justify the inclusion of this kind of knowledge into valid knowledge.

As regards the nature of knowledge, there are three main theories held by different systems of Indian Philosophy. According to the Naiyāyikas, knowledge is an attribute of *Ātman*. The Sāṁkhya and the Yoga consider knowledge to be the modification of the buddhi. Buddhi is material in nature and the supposition further leads to the conclusion that the knowledge also is material in nature. The Bauddhas and the Mīmāṁsakas describe knowledge as an activity. In its most comprehensive sense the knowledge can be said to be the cognition of the objects.

The term *pramāṇa* derivatively means the extraordinary cause of valid knowledge (*pramākaraṇa*). One attains valid knowledge of object through the means of valid knowledge. All the systems of Indian philosophy agree in respect of literal meaning as well as the function or the purpose of *pramāṇa* that it is conducive to the valid knowledge. There is, however, divergence of opinion about the exact nature of the *karaṇa* of valid knowledge. A *karaṇa* is generally conceived as a special cause in producing a particular effect. The speciality of *karaṇa*, however, is variously interpreted by different systematists.

According to the Bauddhas and the Jainas, *pramāṇa* is of the nature of knowledge. Amongst various definitions of *pramāṇa* offered by the Jaina logicians it is commonly accepted that the pramāṇa reveals itself as well as its object.[21] The Bauddhas also define *pramāṇa* as the knowledge which is not contradicted.[22]

The Mīmāṁsakas also hold that *pramāṇa* is the knowledge itself,[23] but they differ from the above-mentioned schools in two respects. Firstly the knowledge, according to the Mīmāṁsakas, unlike the Jainas, is the act or process, and secondly the result of knowledge according to the Mīmāṁsakas, unlike the above two schools, is distinct from the knowledge. The Mīmāṁsakas hold that the result of knowledge is the rise of the notion of cognisedness belonging to the object of knowledge.[24]

The Naiyāyikas explain the term *karaṇa* in the sense of that which is the most conducive to the production of the effect. There is, however, difference of opinion regarding the nature of *karaṇa* between the old and the new Naiyāyikas, which results in the divergence regarding the nature of *pramāṇa* as well. According to the old Naiyāyikas, the *karaṇa* is a cause which is peculier and operative *vyāpāravadasādhāra ṇaṁ kāraṇaṁ*. Here, the term *asādhāraṇa* (peculiar) distinguishes *karṇa* from other causes while the term *vyāpāravat* excludes the other objects of its genus which are not operative at the time of producing the effect but have the potentiality to do so. For example, even among the causes of pot, the sticks which are not operative at the time of producing the pot are excluded from the domain of karaṇa by the term operative. The modern Naiyāyikas, on the other hand, define karaṇa as the cause which is invariably and immediately followed by the product (*phalāyogavyavacchinnaṁ Kāraṇam*). Thus, *karaṇa*, according to the ancient Naiyāyikas is of the nature of the substance while according to the modern Naiyāyikas it is of the nature of operation (***vyāpāra***) **itself**. For example, in case of cutting the wood with **an axe the** *karaṇa* according to the ancient Naiyāyikas, is the **axe itself** while according to the modern Naiyāyikas it is the operation of the axe. In this way, the *karaṇa* in the case of perception, inference, upamāna and verbal testimony is the senses, the knowledge of probans (*liṅga*) or invariable concomitance *(vyāpti)*, the knowledge of similarity and word respectively according to old Naiyāyikas while according to the modren Naiyāyikas it is the sense-object contact, consideration (*parāmarśa*), the remembrance of the statement of the reliable person and the utternace of the authoritative person respectively.[25] Among the Naiyāyikas also Jayantabhaṭṭa does not accept the normal view of his school, and defines *pramāṇa* as the totality of causal conditions. The *pramāṇa* according to Jayantabhaṭṭa is the totality of all the sentient and non-sentient factors which lead to the knowledge of an object which is in turn different from illusion and doubt.[26] Jayantabhaṭṭa is aware of the possible objections against the definition and tries to alleviate them. Firstly, the word *pramāṇa* refers to the *karaṇa*. The nature of *karaṇa* involves the idea of its superiority over the ordinary means. Hence, it requires comparision with other means and this would not hold good if all the means are included into *pramāṇa*.[27] Secondly, if the totality of causal conditions is taken to be the *pramāṇa*, it would include the object and the subject of knowledge also into the category of parmāṇa and such it would jeopardise the Nyāya position that all elements in epistemology can be finally classified into the subject, the object, the means and the process of knowledge.[28] Moreover, some objects which are not directly related to the process of knowing would be called *pramāṇa* but actually without the relation to the process they would not be *karaṇa* at all.[29] Thirdly, such a notion would go against our experience. Nothing except the *karaṇa* is used in the third case affix. No one is found saying that the perceives the object with the totality of causal conditions of perception. On the contrary, people in general are found experiencing that they know the object through their eyes or with a lamp.[30]

Jayantabhaṭṭa alleviates all these objections thus. As to the first objection, he replies that there arises no question of comparison in the totality of causal conditions. The *karaṇa* of knowledge is that the presence of which is invariably followed by the rise of knowledge and the absence of which results into the absence of knowledge. All the causes are possessed of this characteristic and, hence, there is no cause in the totality which is devoid of the nature of the means of knowledge.[31] Replying to the second objection, Jayantabhaṭṭa says that the totality also works through the process of all the conditions included under it. Hence, the karaṇa is not devoid of process in this case also. Moreover, the fourfold division into knower, etc., also is possible when they are invariably connected with the process of knowledge.[32] As to the last objection Jayantabhaṭṭa replies that the totality is never used indepedent of the total members. That is why, it does not take third case affix. The usage thruogh third case affix is permitted in case of the visual organ or the lamp when the nature of producing the knowledge belonging to the totality is attributed to them. The same holds good in the case of the common experience of the usage like 'one cooks with a pot' etc.[33]

The Sāṃkhya-Yoga concept of pramāṇa is different from all these. Patañjali holds that *pramāṇa* is the function of Citta (*cittavṛtti*).[34] The Yuktidipikā states that since the Citta is one, the *pramāṇa* is one only.[35] It is through limiting adjuncts that it is said to be threefold.[36] Vācaspati Miśra also accepts the usually accepted meaning of pramāṇa as the means of valid knowledge. He, however, offers two definitions of *pramā* which imply two different opinions regarding the nature of pramāṇa also. He defines pramā as the modification of *Citta* (*cittavṛtti*) the object of which is not either doubtful (*sandigdha*), contradictory (*viparita*) or known (*adhigata*).[37] The pramāṇa as the means of that will be sense-object contact, etc. He gives an alternate definition of *parmā* as the apprehension of the *Puruṣa* which results from the modification of the *buddhi*.[38] In this case, the *pramāṇa* will be the modification of the *buddhi* itself. Vijñānabhikṣu explains it more vividly. When the result of knowledge is considered to be located in the *buddhi* the *pramāṇa* is the sense-object contact, etc., and when the result of knowledge is considered to be located in the puruṣa the *pramāṇa* is the function of the *buddhi* itself.[39] Vijñānabhikṣu also makes it clear that the use of *pramāṇa* with refernce to the senses, is always indirect.[40]

Regarding the number of the *pramāṇas* also different schools of Indian philosophy adopted a divergent scheme. The number of the *pramāṇas* accepted by them differ from one to nine. The Cārvākas accept Perception only as a single means of knowledge. The Vaiśeṣikas and the Buddhists recognise two-Perception and Inference. Śāṁkhya, Yoga, and the Viśiṣṭādvaita, Dvaita, Śuddhādvaita and the Dvaitādvaita schools of Uttaramīmāṁsā recognise Perception, Inference and the Verbal testimony as the three means of knowledge. The Naiyāyikas recognise the above three with an addition of Upamāna as the fourth. The Prābhākara school of Pūrvamīmāṁsā adds *arthāpatti* (presumption) to it. The Bhāṭṭa school of Pūrvamīmāṁsā and the Advaita school of Uttara-mīmāṁsā recognise the above with the addition of *anupalabdhi*. The Paurāṇikas admit the above six with the addition of *sambhava* (inclusion), *aitihya* (tradition) and pratibhā (imagination).

Footnotes :

1. कः पुनरयं न्याय ? प्रमाणैरर्थपरीक्षणम् ।

N.B. 1.1.

2. प्रमाणमविसंवादिज्ञानम्; अविसंवादनशब्दनिरुक्तिः । अर्थक्रियास्थितिः... ।

P.V. 1.2.

3. प्रापकं ज्ञानं प्रमाणम् ।

N.B.T., p. 4

4. अविसंवादित्वं चाभिमतार्थक्रियासमर्थार्थप्रापणशक्तिकत्वं न तु प्रापणमेव प्रतिबन्धातिसम्भवात् ।

T.S.P.

5. तद्वति तत्प्रकारकानुभवो यथार्थः। सैव प्रमेत्युच्यते।

Tarkas., p. 34.

6. प्रमाणमनुभूतिः।

P.P., p. 124

7. यथार्थं प्रमाणम्।

Pra. P. p.9

8. यथार्थज्ञानं प्रमा। तद्वति तत्प्रकारकत्वं यथार्थत्वम्।

Śrutyantakalpavalli, p. 91

9. निश्चयो यथार्थानुभवः। अयमेव प्रमेति व्यवह्रियते। याथार्थ्यं चार्थानतिवर्तित्वम्।

P.R.K. p.18

10. यथावस्थितव्यवहारानुगुणं ज्ञानं प्रमेति।

N.P., p. 36, also Y.M.D., p.3

11. प्रमात्वमनधिगताबाधितविषयज्ञानत्वम्।

V.P., p.19

12. तत्र स्मृतिव्यावृत्तं प्रमात्वमनधिगताबाधितविषयज्ञानत्वम्, स्मृतिसाधारणं त्वबाधितविषयज्ञानत्वम्।

V.P., p. 19

13. कारणदोषबाधकज्ञानरहितमगृहीतग्राहि ज्ञानं प्रमाणामिति।

S.D., p. 123

14. तच्चासन्दिग्धाविपरीतानधिगतविषया चित्तवृत्तिः।

S.T.K.5.

15. समासतो द्वे विद्ये—विद्या चाविद्या चेति।

P.B., p. 170

16. निःसन्दिग्धाबाधिताध्यवसायात्मिका प्रतीतिर्विद्या, तद्विपरीता चाविद्येति।

N.K., p. 414

17. स्वपरव्यवसायि ज्ञानं प्रमाणम्।

P.N.T. 1,2.

18. वस्तुतथाभावग्राहकत्वं निश्चयात्मकत्वेन...

P.K.M., p. 27

19. प्रमाणं स्वपराभासि बाधाविवर्जितम्।

N.A.V.1.2.

20. प्रमाणमविसंवादिज्ञानमनधिगतार्थाधिगमलक्षणत्वात्।

A.S., p. 175

21. C.F. fn. 17 and 20

22. Cf. fn. 2 and 3
23. अगृहीतग्राहि ज्ञानं प्रमाणमिति प्रमाणलक्षणं सूचितम्।

S.D., p. 123

24. Cf. N.M., pp. 15-16
25. Cf. Y.V. ATHALE'S notes to Tarkas, pp. 187-9
26. अव्यभिचारिणीमसन्दिग्धार्थोपलब्धिं विदधती बोधाबोधस्वभावा सामग्री प्रमाणम्।

N.M., p. 12

27. करणसाधनोऽयं प्रमाणशब्दः करणं च साधकतमं तमबर्थश्चातिशयः, स चापेक्षिकः सामग्र्याश्चैकत्वात्तदतिरिक्तसाधकान्तरानुपलम्भात्किमपेक्षमस्या अतिशयं ब्रूमः।

N.M., Part I, p. 12

28. एवं च यदुच्यते प्रमाता प्रमाणं प्रमेयं प्रमितीति चतसृषु विधासु तत्त्वं परिसमाप्यते इति तद् व्याहन्यते।

N.M., Part I, p. 12

29. ननु किमपेक्षं सामग्र्याः करणत्वमिति।

N.M., Part I, p. 12

30. न ह्येवं वक्तारो भवन्ति लौकिकाः सामग्र्याः पश्याम इति तु किं तु दीपेन पश्यामः चक्षुषा निरीक्षामहे इत्याचक्षते।

N.M., I, p. 12

31. N.M., Part I, p. 12
32. N.M., Part I, p. 13
33. N.M. Part I, p. 13
34. प्रमाणविपर्ययविकल्पनिद्रास्मृतयः।

Y.S. 16

35. तदेकमेव, बुद्धेरेकत्वाभ्युपगमात्।
36. उपाधिवशात्तु भिन्नमाश्रीयते प्रत्यक्षमनुमानमित्यादि।

Y.D. 4

37. तच्चासन्दिग्धाविपरीतानधिगतविषया चित्तवृत्तिः।

S.T.K. 5

38. बोधश्च पौरुषेयफलं प्रमा।

S.T.K. 5

39. अत्र यदि प्रमारूपं फलं पुरुषनिष्ठमात्रमुच्यते, तदा बुद्धिवृत्तिरेव प्रमाणम्। यदि च बुद्धिनिष्ठमात्रमुच्यते, तदा तूक्तेन्द्रियसन्निकर्षादिरेव प्रमाणाम्।

S.P.B. 1.87

40. चक्षुरादिषु तु प्रमाणव्यवहारः परम्परयैव सर्वथेति भावः।

S.P.B. 1.87

CHAPTER II

Nyāya Concept of Upamāna

The Nyāya system aims at providing path for liberation which is attained through the knowledge of the objects.[1] The knowledge is aquired through four means of knowledge-Partyakṣa, Anumāna, Upamāna and Śabda. Upamāna, in brief, is the means of knowing denotative relation between a word and certain class of objects through the intermediary knowledge of similarity, dissimilarity or particular characteristics conveyed by the authoritative statment. There are the following factors in Upamāna: the authoritative statement, the indirect knowledge of similarity, the recollection of the sense of the authoritative statement and, the resultant knowledge. For example, a city-dweller familiar with the cow but unfamiliar with the object denoted by the word *gavaya* hears from a reliable forest-dweller that the gavaya is an animal resembling a cow. Then, he happens to go to the forest and comes across such an animal. He perceives its striking similarity to the cow. Then, he recollects the sense of the statement of the forest-dweller and comes to know that the object before him is denoted by the word *gavaya*.

Gautama defines Upamāna as the means of cognising some (unknown) object (*sādhyasādhana*) through its similarity to a well known object (*prasiddhasādharmyāt*).[2]

From Gautama's definition of *pramāṇa* it is difficult to ascertain what he exactly considers as the nature of *pramāṇa*.

He is not strict about the differentiation into the means and the resultant knowledge while defining the *pramāṇa*. In the case of perception he takes the *pramāṇa* in the sense of resultant knowledge.[3] In the case of verbal testimony he seems to take the term pramāṇa in the sense of the means.[4] In the present case, however, the problem is more complicated. Here, the word *sādhyasādhana* can be interpreted in two ways: (i) the means of establishing and (ii) the result of establishing. The former meaning is accepted by Vātsyāyana and Uddyotakara while the latter is accepted by Vācaspati Miśra. If the earlier interpretation is accepted, Upamāna will mean a means of knowledge and the term *prasiddhasādharmyāt* becomes the basis for the words denoting means in the *sūtra* since the word *prasiddhasādharmya* also denotes the means of knowledge which is further denoted by the term *sādhana*. If the latter interpretation is accepted, the term *prasiddhasādharmyāt* serves as a means and comes nenarer to the probans in inference and, hence, it will be difficult to distinguish it from inference.

To overcome such difficulties the commentators followed by Vātsyāyana interpret the sūtra in their own way. Agian, Gautama uses the terms *sādhana* and *sādhya* which give an inpression that he considers *pramāṇa* as a means of proving an object. However, his definition of perception implies that *pramāṇa* is the means of knowing an object. Therefore, we should understand the term *sādhya* in the sense of the object to be known and the term sādhana in the sense of means of knowledge. To alleviate the above-mentioned undesirable contingency of the recurrence of means in the definition, we should further consider the *sādhana* expressed in the form of assertion of the authoritative person, and similarity to a well known object as the basis of Upamāna. Perhaps, having such an idea in mind Vātsyāyana interprets the *sūtra* that Upamāna as means is the assertion of the authoritative person.

Gautama was aware of the difficulty as to which kind of similarity should be considered as well known. He realises that the opponent may criticise his view on the ground that similarity is understood in terms of degree and the degree of similarity, i.e., perfect partial or *great* is not able to establish something.[5] Hence, Gautama states that Upamāna does not depend upon the degrees of quantity of similarity. What is required is only the similarity of a unknown object to a well known object.[6] Uddyotakara further explains that this kind of well known similarity may be perfect, partial or great. It will surely yield the result. We get the knowledge of the operation through perfect similarity of two operations as the battle between Rāma and Rāvaṇa is like Rāma and Rāvaṇa only. The result of Upamāna is received through great similarity as the buffallo so the cow, where one suggests the similarity between the two with respect of their power. The partial knowledge also leads to the knowledge through Upamāna. For example, when one desires to know the nature of the existence of the mountain Meru, he is told that as the existence of mustard seed, so the exsitence of mountain Meru.' Thus, the similarity in terms of perfect, partial or great does not present some difficulty.[7]

We find in the Nyāyabhāṣya of Vātsyāyana a vague difference between Upamāna as means and the Upamiti, the knowledge resulting from it. While explaining the *sūtra* he states that the Upamāna is the definite knowledge of an object sought to be definitely known through its similarity with a well known object.[8] But he further differentiates between Upamāna as means of knowledge and Upamiti as a resultant knowledge. The *sūtrakāra* does not state anything about the nature of resultant knowledge. It is Vātsyāyana who gives a clear cut exposition of the resultant knowledge. It is deduced from his statement that the purpose of Upamāna is the knowledge of the relation of the name with the corresponding object (*samākhyā*).[9]

Vātsyāyana makes an innovation in explaining the function of Upamāna as a means of knowledge. He considers the assertion *yathā gauḥ, tathā gavayaḥ* (as the cow, so the gavaya) as the Upamāna.[10] Thus analysed, the explanation of Vātsyāyana suggests that the *karaṇa* is the authoritative statement, the *avāntara vyāpāra* is the recollection of the sense of the authoritative statement and the Upamiti is the knowledge of the relation of the name with the denotation.[11] Thus, Vātsyāyana seems to hold that the causes of Upamāna are the memory of the assertion of the authoritative person and the perception of the animal, while the most efficient among them is the authoritative statement itself.

Vātsyāyana offers two more examples of Upamāna. A person is asked by the doctor to bring the medicinal herbs called *Mudgaparṇī* and *Māṣaprṇī* and is told that the *Mudgaparṇī* is like Mudga and the Māṣaparṇī is like *Māṣa*. The person desirous of collecting these herbs goes to the forest and comes across the herbs resembling *Māṣa* and *Mudga*. Through the Upamāna that the *Māṣaparṇī* is like the *Māṣa* and *Mudgaparṇī* is like Mudga he comes to ascertain that the herbs before him are *Māṣaparṇī* and *Mudgaparṇī*.[12]

Uddyotakara clearly differentiates between the means of knowledge and the resultant knowledge. He analyses the nature of Upamāna in a different manner. The term *prasiddhasādharmya*, according to him, denotes the object having well known similarity (*prasiddhaṁ sādharmyaṁ yasya*) or which has got the similarity with a well known object (*prasiddena vā sādharmyaṁ yasya)*. The upamiti is the knowledge through that.[13] Here, one may get the impression that simply the *gavaya* or the perception of it is the Upamāna according to Uddyotakara and this may turn the process of rise of upamiti unintelligible. But, here the *gavaya* is not merely the *gavaya* but that endowed with the similarity with the cow. The perceiver, in fact, sees the similarity. The similarity, however, is the quality of *gavaya* related to it through the relation of inherence. Hence, the statement of Uddyotakara comes to mean the perception of the similarity existing in the *gavaya*.

Like Vātsyāyana, he considers the object of Upamāna as the knowledge of the name and its denotation.[14] He explains the process of Upamāna thus. When one hears from someone that the *gavaya* is like a cow and thus when the similarity of cow and *gavaya* becomes well known, he himself sees the similarity between cow and *gavaya*. Then he comes to know the relation of the term *gavaya* to its denotation.[15]

Here, we find a difference of opinion between the *Bhāṣya* and the *Vārttika*. There is no difference regarding the nature of resultant knowledge for according to both the resultant knowledge is the relation of the name with its denotation. However, there is a clear-cut difference regarding the means of cognition, which further results into the difference regarding the process in cognition. The *karaṇa* is the authoritative statement according to the *Bhāṣya* but the perception of similarity according to Uddyotakara. Moreover, according to the *Bhāṣya* the similarity is apprehended through the recollection of the sense of the authoritative statement while according to the Vārttikakāra the similarity is directly perceived.

Uddyotakara further feels that the mere knowledge of similarity cannot lead to the knowledge of the relation of the name with a particular class of objects. It is experienced in our common life that one does not necessarily know the name of the object the similarity of which is comprehended with some other object. Therefore, Uddyotakara adds that it is not merely the knowledge of similarity which leads to the knowledge of the name and the named but this knowledge should be associated with the revival of the impression caused by the sense of the authoritative statement.[16] Thus, Uddyotakara correlates the authoritative statement and knowledge of similarity. Vācaspati Miśra states that the above statement of

Uddyotakara brings out the sense implicitly expressed by the *sūtrakāra*. He explains that the term *prasiddhasādharmyāt* used for defining Upamāna in the *sūtra* includes both. The knowledge of the similarity is of two kinds: derived through perception and that derived through verbal testimony. The earlier is exemplified as after perceiving the *gavaya* directly one obsreves that the object before him is qualified by the similarity to the cow. The latter is derived through the assertion like 'as the cow, so the *gavaya*'. Thus, the knowledge derived through perception and assisted by that derived through the authoritative statement is the cause of understanding the denotative relation.[17] He seems to understand Upamāna as a means of denotative relation through the knowledge of similarity assisted by the authoritative statement.

Uddyotakara makes furhter innovation by introducing the element of *vaidharmya* (dissimilarity) as the basis of Upamāna. He thinks that the expression *sādharmya* is symbolic in the *sūtra* and includes *vaidharmya* as well.[18]

Vācaspati Miśra is particular in understanding the Upamāna strictly in the sense of *Karaṇa* (means). He suggests that the word *yataḥ* should be inserted in the *sūtra* forming the defination of Upamāna so that it should without doubt be applicable to the *Karaṇa* (means) only.[19] He shows the significance of the words of *sūtra* forming the definition. Merely the expression *sādhyasādhanam* cannot form the definition because it would apply to the other means of knowledge and also to the means of pleasure, pain , etc. Hence, the world *prasiddhasādharmyāt* forms the essential part of the definition.[20] Thuogh Upamāna may be defined as *prasiddhasādharmyam-upamānam* because the sense of instrumentality would be denoted by the term Upamāna which is a specific means of knowledge, yet the word *sādhyasādhana* is used in the definition to exclude Upamānābhāsa.[21]

Vācaspati Miśra further adds that the term *sādharmya* is used elliptically for the properties in general. The Upamiti can as well be derived through the unique characterisics. The person from north India tells a person of south India that a camel is an animal which is ugly in looking, has a very long and crooked neck and long lips, and lives on hard and sharp thorns. After that, the person of south India comes across such an animal in north India and comes to understand that this is the object denoted by the term camel. This is also a case of Upamāna.[22] Vācaspati Miśra tries to trace the authority for his supposition to the statement of the Bhāṣya that in this way other things are known as objects of Upamāna in our day-to-day life.[23]

Jayantabhaṭṭa finds a divergence of opinion among his predecessors regarding the nature of Upamāna. Motivated by this divergence of views he takes into account the views of his predecessors under two heads : earlier and contemporary. He presents the view of the earlier Naiyāyikas as follows. The Upamāna is the authoritative statement which enlightens the similarity which the unknown object bears to a known object and which aims at ascertaining the denotative relation between a name and its denotation. For example, a city-dweller who does not know the nature of *gavaya* asks a forest-dweller what is the nature of *gavaya*. The forest-dweller replies 'as the cow so the *gavaya*'. This sentence is the Upamāna. It informs of the similarity which the unknown object bears to the known object and leads to the knowledge that the word denotes the *gavaya* class.[24]

The contemporary logicians also, like the earlier logicians, hold that Upamāna generates the knowledge of the denotative relation. However, the Upamāna, according to them, is the perceptual knowledge of the similarity which the unknown object bears to the well known one. This, according to them, should be accepted as a distinct means of knowledge because it leads to the cognition of some unknown object, thuogh in itself it is cognised through the senses. The case is analogous to the perceptual knowledge of smoke which leads to the cognition of fire. A city-dweller who has heard the authoritative statement rambles in the forest and comes across an animal similar to the cow. Then, he recollects the statement of the forest-dweller and comes to know that the animal is denoted by the word *gavaya*.[25] In this way, the resultant knowledge of denotative relation and the proximate cause of such a relation is called Upamāna. He records the definition offered by Vātsyāyana under the earlier head and that by Uddyotakara under the latter. Jayanta's main contribution is to wage a fierce intellectual warfare with the opponents the views of the Naiyāyikas. He alleviates the objections levelled against the earlier and the contemporary logicians.

Thus, Gautama and Vātsyāyana regarded Upamāna at of one kind only, i.e., based on similarity. Uddyotakara introduces another basis of Upamāna, viz., dissimilarity and it comes to be of two kinds. Vācaspati Miśra further introduces statement of characteristics also as the basis of Upamāna and thus, it comes to be of three kinds. The later texts of the Naiyāyikas maintain that Upamāna is of three kinds: (i) *sādharmyopamāna* (Upamāna through similarity), (ii) *vaidharmyopamāna*... (Upamāna through dissimilarity) and (iii) *dharmamātropamāna* (Upamāna through mere properties)[26]. The *sādharmyopamāna* is the means of knowing the unknown denotative relation through a description in terms of its similarity to some well known object, just as the name of the animal *gavaya* is known through the authoritative statement propounding the similarity to the cow. A person hears the authoritative statement 'as the cow, so the *gavaya*', and goes to the forest and recollects the statement (at the sight of the *gavaya*). His ascertainment (or investigation) of the application of the name *gavaya* to the animal similar to the cow through which the *gavaya* bears to the cow is a case of Upamāna through the similarity.[27] The *vaidharmyopamāna* is the means when the name of the object to be known is conveyed in terms of its dissimilarity to a well known object as 'the horse is the animal which has the dissimilar hoofs to the cow. A person asks the specialist about the form of a horse. The specialist tells him that it does not have two hoofs like a cow. He recollects the above statement at the sight of the horse and ascertains the application of the name horse to the animal through the dissimilarity which the horse bears to the cow in respect of having one hoof.[28] Or, it may be illustrated as follows : when one asks about the form of earth and is told by some specialist that the earth is having dissimilar properties to the water and ascertians the application of the name earth to the object through the perception of such an object and the recollection of the statement informing of the dissimilar properties, it becomes a case of the knowledge of the denotative relation through dissimilarity.[29] The *dharmamātropamāna* is that where the object is cognised through the statement of peculiar characteristics as the camel is known through the description of its peculiar characteristics as 'the camel is an animal having long neck, projecting lips, and eats the thorns.'[30] Or, as the earth is known through the statement that the earth is that which has the smell as its peculiar characteristic.[31]

Gautama's definition of Upamāna leaves it unexplained what he exactly intends as the purpose of Upamāna. According to Diṅnāga, Gautama postulates Upamāna to cognise the similarity which *gavaya* bears to the cow or to cognise the *gavaya* as qualified by its similarity to the cow, in the example given by the Naiyāyikas.[32] R.D. Randale thinks that Diṅnāga brings out the correct purport of the *sūtra*.[33] The later commentators of the *sūtra*, however, do not accept the interpretation of the *sūtra* offered by *Diṅnāga*. Vātsyāyana is the first commentator who clarifies the idea of practical utility of Upamāna. He points out that the Upamāna helps to collect the medicinal herbs like *Mudgaparṇī* and *Māṣaparṇī*.[34]

Here, Jayantabhaṭṭa states that Upamāna has no bearing upon the final realisation or final emancipation in the way as the other three means of knowledge have a special service to the purpose of Nyāya. But still, Upamāna is not absolutely useless since it has unique part to play in the performance of a vedic rite which enjoins the killing of a *gavaya*. The *gavaya* cannot be killed if one is not acquainted with it. Moreover, this means of knowledge is servicable to identify the medicinal herbs like *Mudgaparṇī and Māsaparṇī*.[35] Gautama has defined Upamāna with a view to render useful service to all, though it has no bearing upon final emancipation. In fact, the Nyāya system is merely a science of sources of valid knowledge and, therefore, should discuss the means of knowledge only. The objects to be known also serve as the means of achieving the final emancipation. Upamāna helps in acquiring the knowledge of the objects to be known.[36]

The Naiyāyikas spare no pains to establish Upamāṇa as an independent means of knowledge. Gautama realises that the opponent may criticise the view of accepting Upamāna on the ground that similarity is understood in term of degree and the degrees of similarity, i.e., perfect, partial or great is not competent to prove something. Hence, Upamāna being based upon similarity, cannot be a means in establishing something.[37] This seems to be an argument raised by the Cārvākas who reject Upamāna as a means of valid knowledge, though there is no textual support for such a supposition. To this argument, Gautama replies that Upamāna does not depend upon the degree of similarity, what it requires is only the similarity of the unknown object.[38] Uddyotakara further adds that the well known similarity may be perfect, partial or great, it will surely yield the result.[39] Gautama further alleviates an objection that

Upamāna is a case of inference.[40] The later Naiyāyikas further argue that the Upamāna cannot be reduced to the other means of knowledge also. Now we proceed to discuss the views of the systematists who include the Upamāna under some other means, and Naiyāyikas' arguments against such a possibility.

It is admitted by all the systematists except the Cārvākas that the process involved in Upamāna leads to a valid knowledge and as such it cannot be rejected as means of non-valid knowledge. However, the other systems are not perpared to allot an independent status to it. Therefore, they try to reduce it to the other pramāṇas accepted by them. Here, we proceed to discuss first the reasons of non-acceptance of its independent position and the views regarding inclusion of Upamāna under the other pramāṇas, and then to consider the possibility of its inclusion under the other pramāṇas as suggested by other systematists.

There is nothing new cognised by Upamāna. The *gavaya*, in the case of the familiar example, is cognised through perception and similarity is the case of remembrance.[41]

Here, the Naiyāyikas argue that the object of Upamāna is neither the *gavaya* nor the similarity but the combination of the two. It is the *gavaya* qualified by its similarity to the cow which forms the object of Upamāna. This kind of object is neither cognised through perception nor is it the case of remembrance.[42] The argument, states Kumārilbahaṭṭa, is right, but it does not turn the position of Naiyāyikas faultless. It involves other absurdities. Here, it may be asked whether it produces any idea over and above the one expressed in the authoritative statement or not. If the second alternative is accepted, it will not have anything more than remembrance and as such it would not be a means of knowledge at all because it would be the mere repetition to the knowledge already acquired and does not, like remembrance, have some more objective.[43] The acceptance of first alternative turns it into a case of perception. If it is argued that it is not only the object which is conveyed through the authoritative statement but, in addition to it, the form of the *gavaya* qualified by the similarity to the cow which forms the object of Upamāna, it would not be something more than the perception because so long as the cognition arises through sense-object it is the case of perception. The form of *gavaya* and its being qualified by the similarity to the cow are cognised by sense-object contact and, hence, forms the object of perception.[44] The Naiyāyikas come forward with the argument that knowledge of similarity of *gavaya* to the cow certainly exceeds perception in the present case and, therefore, it is not a case of perception. Kumārilabhaṭṭa rejects the plea on the ground that the factor of remembrance which exceeds perception is invalid.[45] Pārthasārathimiśra adds that the invalidity attaches to the part remembered but it does not enter into the part known through perception. The same knowledge can be both valid and otherwise at a time due to the difference of its objects. Hence, the part of knowledge based upon remembrance is invalid while the part based on perception is valid.[46] The knowledge of the authoritative statement regarding similarity does not serve any purpose because such persons who have known the cow and happen to see the *gavaya* come to know the similarity even without the knowledge of the authoritative statement.[47] Here, the Naiyāyikas come forward with the theory that the object of Upamāna is the denotative relation and such knowledge does not arise without knowing the authoritative statement. Kumārilabhaṭṭa strikes the root of the Nyāya theory arguing that the knowledge of denotative relation cannot be the object of Upamāna because it is already cognised through the authoritative statement.[48] The Naiyāyikas may argue that the object of Upamāna in that case, will be the recognition of the fact that a particular word denotes a particular object. The power of denotation (*vācyavācakaśakti*) is beyond the senses and, thus, it is not an object of recognition. To this Kumārilabhṭṭa replies that the knowledge of this type of power is also a case of remembrance.[49] Pārthasārathimiśra further adds that it can also not be argued on the part of the Naiyāyikas that the power being supra sensuous is not the object of perception and is cognised only through infernce. The power is nothing exceeding space and time and since it is not a separate category, it cannot be an object of some distinct means of knowledge. This is simply a case of remembrance[50].

Here, the Naiyāyikas are presented as trying to establish Upamāna as different from perception. The perception depends upon the sense-object contact while Upamāna requires the authoritative statement in addition. This also, states Kumārilabhaṭṭa, does not turn the stand of the Naiyāyikas faultless because the factor of sense-object contact is found in this case as well.[51] Here, it may be observed that Kumārilabhaṭṭa criticises all the points different from his own position on Upamāna. He differs from the Naiyāyikas mainly on the issue of the object of Upamāna, and the nature of resultant knowledge through Upamāna. In brief, the Naiyāyikas cannot explain the object of Upamāna. To establish the existence of some independent means of knowledge there must be some object which can be cognised exclusively through that means. In the absence of such an object the Nyāya theory falls to the ground. Nārāyaṇa adduces the following additional arguments against the theory of the Naiyāyikas. This theory, being mistaken, should be discarded because the knowledge of denotative relation is produced merely by verbal testimony assisted by perception.[52] It is experienced in our common life that the knowledge of the denotative relation is possible through words assisted by perception. For example, after hearing the statement that the merchant has *nava* (nine or new) blankets one goes to the market and after seeing nine blankets with the merchant remembers the sentence and concludes that the purport of the sentence was a particular number and thus, understands the meaning of the sentence.[53] Narāyaṇa further adds that it is also experienced in our day-to-day behaviour that Upamāna is used where there is similarity and not in the case where there are uncommon attributes in general. Even the authoritative statement heard at some other place is well known in case of a sentence declaring common attributes only. Hence, there is no usage of Upamāna through the uncommon attributes of the attributes in general.[54]

Śālikanātha objects to the view of the Naiyāyikas that they cannot explain the nature of Upamāna as a distinct means. In the stock example of the Naiyāyikas, the first knowledge that the *gavaya* is similar to the cow arises through the authoritative statement and is not the result of Upamāna. The knowledge of *gavaya* and its similarity to the cow arising in the man who has gone to the forest are recognition and perception respectively. The understanding that this object is denoted by the word *gavaya* is the inferential knowledge. When a word is used in certain sense, one comes to know the denotative relation with the object. 'After acquiring the knowledge of the denotative relation in the forest, the final cognition 'the name known to me is of that animal only' is the case of remembrance. Thus there is no scope for Upamāna.[55]

The followers of the Advaita school of the Uttara-mīmaṁsā also criticise the Nyāya concept of admitting Upamāna as an independent means of cognising the denotative relation. Ānandapūrṇa states that Upamāna, according to the Naiyāyikas, is the investigation or examination in the object named of the meaning of the sentence containing the name the denotation of which is not yet cognised. For example, one hears from the reliable person that the *gavaya* is similar to a cow and he happens to see a *gavaya* in the forest. Then, he recollects the meaning of the reliable statement and, thus, arises in him the knowledge of the denotative relation. The knowledge of the denotative relation is cognised through Upamāna only. Hence, the Upamāna is a distinct means of knowledge.[56] Objecting to the above view, Ānandapūrṇa states that it is reckless statement that such a relation cannot be cognized through any other means of knowledge. Such a relation can be known through Inference. The form of syllogism may be put in the following manner. The word is the conveyer of the object in the sense of which it is used without taking recourse to some other power of denotation, as the word cow denotes the cow class. The word *gavaya* is used in the sense of the class resembling the cow without taking recourse to other power of denotation. Hence, the word *gavaya* denotes the *gavaya* class.[57]

The Viśiṣṭādvaita school of Uttaramīmaṁsā also holds that it is needless for the Naiyāyikas to postulate Upamāna for the purpose of knowing the denotative relation. Vedāntadeśika states that the Upamāna is not different from verbal testimony. It is a statement which conveys the denotative relation through similarity, dissimilarity or peculiar properties.[58] Nor is it correct to hold that Upamāna is the means of recognition of the object meant by the authoritative statement because in this case also the denotative relation is already cognised.[59] The factor of restricting the use of a certain word in a certain sense, viz. similarity, was also known through the authoritative statement and it becomes clear at the sight of the *gavaya*.[60] The unclear image of an object cannot be denied. On the contrary, such cognition is supported by our common experience. Nor can it be argued that the denotative relation is not cognised through such an image. The denotative relation in case of the supra sensuous divinities like Rāma is cognised through such a general or the unclear image.[61] Meghanādasūri further establishes that the Upamāna as a means invisaged by the Naiyāyikas, is the perception of similarity and it comes to be a case of recognition.[62] Otherwise, the Naiyāyikas will have to admit some other means for such a cognition 'this is the same Devadatta.'[63] The resultant knowledge is simply a case of remembrance since the denotative relation between the word *gavaya* and its denotation was already cognised through the authoritative statement.[64] Moreover, if the similarity is the means, the similarity being manifold would require many pramāṇas to determine the denotative relation in case of several objects.[65] Śrīnivāsadāsa is in favour of including it under any of the perception, inference and verbal testimony in accordance with the stress laid upon the particular aspect of it. It is a case of inference if the stress is laid upon the denotative relation as conveyed through the invariable concomitance.[66] It is a case of perception when the stress is laid upon the perception of similarity cognised earlier,[67] and it becomes a case of verbal testimony if the stress is laid upon the authoritative statement.[68]

The Dvaita school of Uttaramīmāṁsā also objects to the independent status of Upamāna. Jayatīrtha states that the purpose of Upamāna is served by inference only.[69] It is also not correct to argue that the form of invariable concomitance, etc., postulated in case of the syllogistic form for Upamāna differs from that found in the formal type of inference which is supposed to be of many kinds due to the form of invariable concomitance and hence the Upamāna may also be taken as a particular type of inference.[70] Moreover, like inference, the Upamāna envisaged by the Naiyāyikas also depends upon the similarity between the *vyāpti* and *pakṣadharmatā*.[71] So, it is needless to accept Upamāna as a means of valid knowledge.

The Śuddhādvaita school of Uttaramīmāṁsā also does not find the need of accepting Upamāna as an independent means for cognising the denotative relation through similarity, etc. The purpose of Upamāna is served by the cognitive organ in association with the remembrance of similarity conveyed through the authoritative statement.[72] Otherwise, the Naiyāyikas will have to postulate the other means for congnising the perceptible objects which exist but are not observed at a particular time.[73] Nor should it be argued here that there is no operation of the cognitive organs at the time of deciding the denotative relation through Upamāna. The purpose is served by the earlier operation of the cognitive organs the impression of which still persists.[74] If the operation of the cognitive organs is thought to be necessary, it may be considered to be the result of mental operation as it is found in the case of cognising the denotative relation with reference to the words like *Madhukara*.[75] The position is supported by the form of *anuvyasāya* which ascertains the nature of the knowledge and the means of it.[76]

The Dvaitādvaita school of Uttaramīmāṁsā does not approve the independent position of Upamāna. Mukunda Mādhava thinks that the Upamāna is a case of instance which forms a component of the syllogism in inference.[77]

The Buddhists also criticise Nyāya view of Upamāna mainly for the purpose of rejecting it as an independent means of knowledge. Dignāga holds it to be a case of perception or verbal testimony since the knowledge arising out of it can be acquired either through perception or through verbal testimony.[78] Śāntarakṣita argues that the idea of denotative relation arises through the authoritative statement itself and it is remembered at the time of perceiving the object denoted by that name. It would, thus, be a case of remembrance which is not a means valid knowledge at all.[79] Moreover, the Nyāya theory involves the incongruity of infinite number of the means of knowledge since the notion of denotative relation is formed by endless means even apart from similarity.[80] Mokṣākaragupta adds that Upamāna lacks the necessary condition for admitting an independent means of knowledge since it has no object to be cognisesd exclusively through it.[81] It is not logical to postulate the denotative relation as an object of Upamāna. There is no relation such as the denotative relation.[82]

The Jainas also criticise the Nyāya theory mainly with a view to reject it as an independent means of knowledge. Akalaṅka argues if the similarity is the basis for denotative relation, the Naiyāyikas should postulate some other means for the denotative relation through dissimilarity or general characteristics.[83] Moreover, they will have to postulate some additional source for the knowledge 'this is nearer, farther, latter, less or greater than the other.'[84]

The Sāṁkhyas also criticise the Nyāya view on the ground that it is unnecessary to postulate Upamāna as an independent means of knowledge. The *Yuktidīpikā* states that Upamāna is a case of verbal testimony. It cannot be argued that the Upamāna requires similarity as an additional factor since the similarity is only a mode of expression.[85] Like verbal testimony, Upamāna also depends upon the validity of the statement.[86] Moreover; the view that Upamāna leads to the knowledge of denotative relation will lead to accept the indefinite number of the means because all the other types of indications leading to the knowledge of the denotative relation will have to be considered as independent means of knowledge.[87] Vācaspati Miśra's criticism implies that neither the totality of causal conditions nor the resultant knowledge requires Upamāna as an independent source. As to the view of Vātsyāyana, he states that the authoritative statement which serves as a means is a case of verbal testimony because the knowledge arising out of it is a case of *āgama* while the resultant knowledge through Upamāna is inferential in nature.[88]

The Vaiśeṣikas also reject the view of the Naiyāyikas with a view to include Upamāna under inference. The denotative relation is conveyed through verbal testimony and since the verbal testimony is included in inference, it is the case of inference.[89] Śrīdhara adds that the *Karaṇa*, i.e., the authoritative statement accepted by the bhāṣyakāra and the knowledge arising out of it is a case of verbal testimony while the knowledge arising out of the whole process is inferential.[90] Śaṁkaramiśra further holds that Upamāna may be proved as a case of inference directly also.[91]

Among the Naiyāyikas also Bhāsarvajña rejects the normal Nyāya view of admitting Upamāna as a distinct means of knowledge. He includes the Upamāna envisaged by the syncretist Naiyāyikas under verbal testimony. If the Upamāna is held to be a distinct means of knowledge on the basis of conveying comparison, it will involve undesirable contingency of admitting indefinite number of means of knowledge because every individual object would require a distinct *pramāṇa* for the determination of the denotative relation.[92] To defend their theory the Naiyāyikas may argue here that in such cases there is an implicit understanding that the term cow applies to all animals of the same class. To this, Bhāsarvajña replies that even in case of Upamāna there is the implication that an animal that resembles a cow bears that particular name.[93] He further tries to establish that this does not go against the view of the *sūtrakāra* since the *sūtrakāra* does not intend to establish the Upamāna as a distinct means but mentions it as it is serviceable to establish the validity of verbal testimony.[94] Gautama discusses it only to show that like presumption it is valid but is included under other means of knowledge.[95] Its distinction from inference established in the *sūtras* does not establish its distinction form verbal *testimony* also.[96] *Sūtrakāra's* enumeration of the *pramāṇas* as four and not as three shows that here, as at some other places, the *sūtrakāra* does not state his view carefully.[97]

As regards the inclusion of Upamāna under other *pramāṇas* the view of different systems may be summarised thus. As stated above, there are three elements in Nyāya concept of Upamāna : (i) communication about the denotative relation through the authoritative statement, (ii) observation of a certain object as resembling the one perceived earlier and (iii) the resultant knowledge. There is the difference of opinion among the Naiyāyikas themselves regarding the status of the first two. Vātsyāyana lays stress on the first whole Uddyotakara lays more stress on the second. This has given rise to the further difference regarding the *karaṇa* in Upamāna. Vātsyāyana holds that the *karaṇa* in Upamāna is the authoritative sentence itself while Uddyotakara takes *karaṇa* to be the perceptual knowledge of similarity. The nature of resultant knowledge is the same in both the cases.

Some critics of Nyāya have clearly noted the difference and have included these two views under different *pramāṇas.* The other are not so strict about the difference and include both the views under the same *pramāṇa*. Some systematists include it under a single *pramāṇa* while the others consider it a combined process of two or more *pramāṇas*. The grounds of inclusion of Upamāna under other *pramāṇa* are different. Bhāsarvajña seems to take note of Vātsyāyana's view only and includes it under verbal testimony.[98] Udayana in his *Kiraṇāvali* also includes the Nyāya view under verbal testimony.[99] Śrīdhara includes Vātsyāyana's view under verbal testimony and further holds that since verbal testimony is a case of inference the Upamāna is also included under inference.[100] As regards the view of Uddyotakara, Śrīdhara says that it contains three elements : statement of authoritative person, perception of similarity and the resultant knowledge. They can be taken as the case of verbal testimony, perception and inference respectively and consequently Upamāna may be taken to be any of the above three.[101]

The Yuktidīpikā also considers Upamāna to be case of verbal testimony itself.[102] Vācaspati in his *Sāṁkhyatattvakaumudi* favours its inclusion under verbal testimony or the inference when the stress is laid upon the authoritative statement and the resultant knowledge respectively.[103] Gauḍapāda favours its inclusion under verbal testimony.[104] The *Jayamaṅgalā* includes it either under verbal testimony or inference.[105] It clarifies that the knowledge of the denotative relation after hearing the authoritative statement and before seeing the *gavaya* directly, is a case of verbal testimony and the term *gavaya* is applied to the animal *gavaya* through inference.[106] Māṭhara,[107] the *Sāṁkhyacandrikā*[108] and Vijñānabhikṣu[109] include it under inference.

Dignāga, as quoted by Uddyotakara,[110] includes it under perception or verbal testimony. According to Śāntarakṣita Upamāna is a case of memory[111] or inference.[112] The Jainas include it under *pratyabhijñā*.[113] Vedāntadeśika favours its inclusion under verbal testimony[114] while Meghanādasūri takes it as a case of recognition,[115] and Śrīnivāsadāsa says that it can be included under any of the perception, inference and verbal testimony.[116] Jayatīrtha includes it under inference.[117] Puruṣottama considers it as the case of perception.[118]

Upamāna versus Perception

Some authors lay stress upon the element of perception of similarity which is considered to be *karaṇa* of Upamāna by Uddyotakara. They are further aware of the fact of admitting the remembrance of the authoritative statement as additional to it and solve the problem of disproving the criterion of additional factor in their own way. Kumārilabhaṭṭa states that as the knowledge of denotative relation is supposed to issue from perception of similarity, it can very well be a case of perception.[119] He further explains that the element of remembrance is not a valid piece of knowledge.[120] Hence, what induces to the knowledge of denotative realtion is the sense-object contact only. Śrīdhara[121] and Śrīnivāsadāsa[122] also join hands with Kumārilabhaṭṭa. Puruṣottama lays stress upon the perceptual character of Upamāna more elaborately and in a slightly different way. He holds that the purpose of Upamāna can be served by the sense-object contact assisted by the remembrance of the similarity conveyed through the authoritative statement.[123] Thus, he thinks that the object denoted is perceived while the similarity is remembered. If it is admitted to be a case of independent pramāṇa on the ground of the addition of one element of similarity, it would lead to the undesirable contingency .of admitting distinct means for the knowledge of an object which is perceptible but is not perceived at that time.[124] It should not be argued that the above position would not leave the indirect nature of Upamāna. The Upamāna should be taken as a case of direct perception.[125] The Naiyāyikas may again come forward with a plea that the cognitive relation was known through the authoritative statement and it is confirmed through the perception of similarity. To this also Puruṣottama replies that the impression of earlier contact of the cognitive sense with object still persists and there is no need of postulation of a fresh contact.[126] Puruṣottama shows his awareness of over-pervasion of the scope perception and, hence, finally takes Upamāna as a result of mental operation. The denotative relat on is cognised through mental operation as is the case with the denotative relation of the words like *madhukara.*[127] Puruṣottama supports his view with the help of another argument based upon *anuvyavasāya* which determines the nature of knowledge. In the present case, the *anuvyavasāya* arises in the form 'I know the object as denoted by certain word.'[128] Such a knowledge requires the mental operation as a means and thus, there is no scope for Upamāna. Diṅnāga, as quoted by Uddyotakara, suggests one of the alternatives to include it under perception When, in the stock example of the

Naiyāyikas, one directly perceives both the cow and the *gavaya*, it is known through sense-object contact that the *gavaya* is similar to the cow.[129]

The Naiyāyikas leave no stone unturned to establish Upamāna as distinct from perception. They strongly opposits inclusion under perception. As to the view of Diṅnāga, Uddyotakara says that it is based upon misunderstanding of the real purpose of Upamāna. Diṅnāga thinks that what is really apprehended through Upamāna is either the resemblance to the cow or the existence of *gavaya* as qualified by the resemblance to the cow. This misunderstanding leads him to reject Upamāna as an independent means of knowledge. If Diṅnāga claims to derive such a meaning from the *sūtras* of Gautama, the criticism is based upon the non-understanding of the correct meaning of the *sūtra*. The purport of the statement of Gautama, however, is that one realises the denotative relation through well-known similarity.[130] Jayantabhaṭṭa rejects the perceptual character of Upamāna more elaborately. He states that the view of the opponent is based upon considering the perception of similarity which the *gavaya* bears to the cow as a *karaṇa* in Upamāna. Here, the opponent ignores the fact that perception of the mediate fact does not turn the concerned means into perception. The case is analogous to inference which is regarded as an independent means of knowledge, though the mediate fact is an object of perception. The perception of smoke in a hill leads to the inferential knowledge of the unperceived fire. Similarly, the perception of *gavaya* gives rise to the knowledge of the denotative relation.[131] Moreover, the scope of Upamāna is not covered by perception. In the case of perception the stress is laid upon the knowledge of an object while Upamāna gives rise to the knowledge of denotative relation in case of an object which was not perceived earlier.[132] Udayana adds that the purpose of Upamāna, viz. The cognition of the denotative relation, cannot be served by perception because otherwise there would arise the undesirable contingency of rise of such a cognition even in the case of the person who has not heard the authoritative statement earlier.[133]

Upamāna versus Inference

Some esystematists include Upamāna under inference. They lay stress upon the fact that the element of resultant knowledge of denotative relation can be attained through inference also. The Niayāyikas hold that one knows the word denoting certain class of word from the authoritative statement and with the perception of a mark of similarity, etc., in the object denoted by that word he applies it to that object. In this way, the Upamāna serves the purpose of knowing the denotative relation. However, the other systematists think that this can very well be a case of inference also. Their grounds of its inclusion under inference are divergent in many respects. Among the Vaiśeṣikas, Praśastapāda states that in the stock example of the Naiyāyikas the knowledge of the denotative relation is based upon the use of the word *gavaya* in the sense of animal *gavaya* and, hence, it can very well be reduced to inference.[134] Śrīdhara suggests one of the alternatives to include Upamāna under inference and holds that the knowledge of the denotative relation in the stock example of the Naiyāyikas is derived through the consistent use of a word in a particular sense. Here, he suggests the form of the syllogism as : the object (present) is denoted by the word *gavaya*, because the word *gavaya* is used with reference to it. The word denotes an object in the sense of which it is consistently used. The word *gavaya* also is consistently used in the sense of animal *gavaya* by the forest-dweller. Therefore, the animal is denoted by the word *gavaya*.[135] Śaṁkaramiśra also favours the inclusion of Upamāna under inference. However, he holds that the denotative relation is known at the time of hearing the authoritative sentence itself. The denotative relation is known through the fact that the object similar to cow and the word *gavaya* conveyed through the authoritative statement refer to the same object. Hence, the object similar to cow should be denoted by the term *gavaya*.[136] Here, the Naiyāyikas may argue, adds Śaṁkaramiśra, that *gavayatva* which determines the use of the term *gavaya* in the sense of animal *gavaya* is not known at the state of hearing the authoritative statement and as such the knowledge of the denotative relation cannot arise. Śaṁkaramiśra alleviates the objection stating that the knowledge of *gavayatva* is possible through a figurative sense and, hence, presents no problem.[137]

Śālikanātha also argues that the Nyāya concept of Upamāna can be reduced to inference and the syllogism can be formed as : the term *gavaya* denotes the animal gavaya because it is used in the sense of the latter. The word denotes an object with reference to which it is used. Thus, one comes to know the denotative relation.[138] Vācaspatimiśra also includes Upamāna under inference. Like Śrīdhara and Śālikanātha, he considers the use of a certain word in a particular sense by experienced persons as a probans but adds a condition 'when there is no function other than direct denotation'. such a purpose is fulfilled by the use of the idea of consistent use employed by Śrīdhara. Vācaspati puts the syllogism like this : the *gavaya* denotes the animal *gavaya*, because it is used in the sense of the latter by experienced persons when there is no function other than direct denotation. When there is no function other than direct denotation, a term used by the experienced person in the sense of a particular object is regarded as denoting that object just as the term cow. The term *gavaya* is used in the sense of an object similar to cow. Therefore, it should be accepted as denothing the animal *gavaya*.[139] Ānandapūrṇa a logician of Advaita Vedānta school also adduces the same argument to include Upamāna under inference.[140] Māṭhara,[141] Vijñānabhikṣu[142] and the *Sāṁkhyacandrikā*[143] also include it under inference but suggest no form of syllogism. The *Jayamaṅgalā* suggests that the denotation of the word *gavaya* is known through the authoritative statement, and after perceiving the animal *gavaya* the term *gavaya* is applied to it through inference. Here, the horns, etc., which are perceived to be similar in the case of cow and *gavaya* serve as a probans for the application of the term *gavaya* to the animal *gavaya*.[144]

Jayatīrtha also advocates the inclusion of Upamāna under inference. He suggests the following process of inference. The subject of enquiry is denoted by the term *gavaya*, because itself a non-cow it is similar to cow, just as a jar by agreement in absence.[145] Rāghavendratīrtha shows the significance of the terms itself a non-cow (*agotve sati*) and similar to cow (*gasadṛśa*). The former wards of the possibility of the application of such inference to the cow which bears the similarity to the other cow and the latter excludes the possibility of the overpervasion of the application of such an inference to the pot, etc.[146]

Jayatīrtha suggests the form of syllogism in case of the sādharmyopamāna only under the impression that it will make it easy to comprehend the syllogism with reference to the other two kinds of Upamāna also.[147] Rāghavendratīrtha mentions the syllogistic form in case of the other two also. The subject of enquiry is denoted by the word horse because it has got one hoof and thus is dissimilar to the cow. The third case will be as the object of enquiry is denoted by the word camel because it possesses long neck, etc., just as a cow by agreement in absence.[148] Jayatīrtha further says that the upholders of Upamāna as an independent means of knowledge may argue that the form of invariable concomitance (*vyāpti*) etc., differ in the case of Upamāna from that found in the actual inference. To this, Jayatīrtha replies that Upamāna is considered to be a particular type of inference. The form of *vyāpti* differs in case of positive (*anvayī*) and negative (*vyatireki*) type of inference, but still they are included under inference. Similarly, in case of Upamāna the vyāpti is of a particular type and thus, does not cease to be a case of inference. Moreover, like inference, the similarity between the *vyāpti* and the *pakṣadharmatā* is required here also. Hence, it cannot be further argued that it is not a case of inference because it establishes a particular fact, viz., the denotative relation.[149] Śāntarakṣita also suggests the inclusion of Upamāna under inference as one of the alternatives. If the stress is laid upon the fact that the words envisage a specific individual, the resultant knowledge becomes a case of inference. The animal which is similar to the cow is denoted by the term *gavaya* just like another *gavaya* present in the mind at the time of learning the denotative relation from a reliable person.[150] Here, the denotation of the name *gavaya* is the probandum, similarity to the cow is the probans, the *gavaya* present in the mind at the time of learning the denotative relation serves as a corroborative instance and the animal *gavaya* which is the subject of enquiry serves as a subject (*pakṣa*).[151] Nor can it be argued here that the *gavaya* was not present at time of learning the denotative relation, otherwise it cannot be known as to with reference to what the convention in the form that it is similar to the cow was made.[152]

The Naiyāyikas leave no stone unterned to disprove the inclusion of Upamāna under inference. Even in the *sūtras* of Gautama we find an attempt to eastablilsh Upamāna as different from inference. Gautama states that the supporters of inclusion of Upamāna under inference may argue that Upamāna is not different from inference because like the latter it gives knowledge of the unpercieved object through the perceived one.[153] Gautama alleviates the objection on the ground that it is not that the purpose of Upamāna is to give rise to the knowledge of unperceived object like *gavaya*.[154] Vātsyāyana explains the argument more vividly. Actually, the Upamāna gives us the knowledge of the denotation when both the cow and the *gavaya* are perceived while inference leads to the knowledge of the unpercieved object through the perceived one. Hence, it is not a case of inference.[155] Gautama further argues that Upamāna, unlike inference, is always expressed in the from 'as .....so......' and hence is not identical with inference which is expressed in terms of relation of grounds and consequence.[156] Vātsyāyana states that in the case of Upamāna it is necessary that the resemblance must be pointed out by some authoritative person but in the case of inference the ground of *vyāpti* may be deduced by one's own experience without such an authoritative statement.[157] Vātsyāyana further adds one more point of difference between Upamāna and inference. Upamāna is always for the sake of another person only while inference is for one's own benefit also. In the case of Upamāna the proposition is made by a person who knows both the members of similarity. It is, therefore, not a case of inference.[158] Vācaspati suggests that the syllogistic form based upon the use of a particular word in the sense of an animal similar to the *gavaya* cannot prove the denotative relation in the given example. Here, the probans may be put as—because the word *gavaya* is used in the sense of an animal similar to cow. However, the *gavayatva* which serves as the cause of the use of the word in the sense of the animal *gavaya* was not cognised through the authoritative statement and hence, the process of Upamāna cannot to put in a faultless syllogism. If the knowledge of *gavaya* is supposed to be acquired by its similarity to the cow, it would involve the fault of inter-dependence. Nor can it be said that the sense of *gavayatva* can be attained metaphorically because the *gavayatva* is not indicated through the similarity to the cow.[159] Jayantabhaṭṭa adds that Upamāna cannot be a case of inference also since, unlike inference, the knowledge arising through Upamāna does not depend upon the positive or the negative invariable concomitance. The invariable concomitance between the word and its denotation was not yet ascertained before deducing it through Upamāna. Thus, the denotative relation is cognised independently of the knowledge of invariable concomitance whereas in the case of inference such an invariable concomitance plays a major role.[160]

Udayāna tries to disprove the inferential character of Upamāna more elaborately. The opponents may include it under inference thus. The word *gavaya* denotes the animal *gavaya* because it is applied to the latter by cultured people when there is no other function of the word than direct denotation *(abhidhā)* just as the word *go* used in the sense of cow by the cultured persons denotes the cow.[161] To this, Udayana replies that here the probans is vitiated by the fallacy of the non-establishment of the reason (*asiddhatva*). The condition for the probans, viz., its application without some other power of denotation cannot be fulfilled until the denotation of the word *gavaya* in the sense of the animal *gavaya* is fully comprehended.[162] And, if the relation is supposed to be known earlier, the very purpose of such an inference would be disturbed.[163] Udayana further presents the opponent arguing that the statement of the authoritative person, viz., that which is similar to a cow is called *gavaya* expresses the case of invariable concomitance (*vyāpti*) and after ascertaining such an invariable concomitance *(vyāpti)* and perceiving the similarity to the cow in the *gavaya* one remembers the invariable concomitance and, thus, reaches the conclusion that the object present is denoted by the term *gavaya*.[164] Udayana controverts the argument on the ground that it is based upon incorrect interpretation of the purpose of the authoritative statement. This would have been the position if the question to the authoritative person is supposed to come from a person who has got the knowledge of the object similar to the cow and now enquires about its denotation. But, actually the quest here refers to the case like this. After knowing the object *gavaya* in general (i.e., without knowing the particular shape) one asks the authoritative person how is this animal.[165] Moreover, here the pervaded (*vyāpya*) is that denoted by the word yat. Hence, the invariable concomitance in the form that whatever is similar to cow is called *gavaya* cannot lead to the desired inference.[166] The opponent may again come forward with a plea that the statement of the authoritative person may be considered as a response to the question regarding the nature of *gavaya* and, thus, it can be a case of inference.[167] Udayana objects to the plea thus. In this way it would be a case of the *kevalavyatireki* (having the counter example only) kind of inference as is found in the case of the general rule regarding the peculiar characteristic of an object. Thus, we would get the counter example only and the form of the *vyatirekavyāpti* would be as that which is not *gavaya* is not similar to cow, as the elephant. However, the counter example also is not yet established. Hence, it cannot be a case of inference.[168] Nor is it correct to take the authoritative statement as a response to the question regarding the probans to infer the denotative relation. In the present case, it is not that the denotative word or the denoted object is cognised and the probans is not yet cognised.[169] The *anuyavasāya* (introspective consciousness) which determines the nature of knowledge also establishes the difference between inference and Upamāna. In inference one feels 'I infer', but in case of Upamāna one feels 'I know from similarity.'[170]

Upamāna Versus Verbal testimony

Some systematists include Upamāna under verbal testimony. Most of these authors take recourse to Vātsyāyana's view according to which the *karaṇa* is the authoritative statement while the others who include Uddyotakara's view of Upamāna under verbal testimony absolutely or as one of the other alternatives lay stress upon the element of authoritative statement.

Bhāsarvajña includes Upamāna under verbal testimony. He thinks that the Upamāna, like the latter, depends upon the authoritative statement. The acceptance of Upamāna as an independent means of knowledge would lead to the undesirable contingency of admitting as many means of knowledge as the objects because each object would require a distinct means for its cognition.[171] He finally concludes that his interpretation brings forth the correct meaning of the statement of the *sūtrakāra*. The author of the sūtras does not intend to establish Upamāna as an independent means of knowledge but mentions it for its seviceableness to prove the validity of verbal testimony.[172] Praśastapāda also includes Upamāna under verbal testimony.[173] Śrīdhara further thinkş that the element of verbal testimony and the knowledge arising of it in case of Uddyotakara's view is also of the nature of verbal testimony.[174] Udayana seems to include the view of Vātsyāyana and Uddyotakara under verbal testimony. He is of the opinion that the nature of the causal condition and the resultant knowledge lead to the same conclusion. The element of similarity which exceeds here does not turn it altogether different from verbal testimony. The denotative relation is known through the essence of *gavaya (gavayatva)* which is conveyed through the authoritative statement itself.[175]

The *Yuktidipikā* holds that in case of Upamāna the knowledge of denotative relation is acquired through the authoritative sentence only.[176] As regards the statement of similarity, the *Yuktidipikā* states that it is merely a mode of expression and, thus, is not a factor for making Upamāna an independent means of knowledge.[177] Otherwise, the other modes like waving the hand and closing the eye would be independent means of knowledge.[178] Moreover, Upamāna like verbal testimony depends upon the fact whether the speaker has visualised the object or not, and upon particular words.[179] Otherwise, knowledge of *gavaya* would arise through the statement 'as the horse, so the *gavaya*'.[180] Moreover, the Naiyāyikas will have to admit some other means of knowledge for the sentences which convey the denotative relation through other elements like description.[181] Vācaspati thinks that the knowledge arising from the statement called Upamāna by Vātsyāyana is verbal in nature and hence, it is not different from verbal testimony.[182] Gauḍapāda favours to include Upamāna under verbal testimony.[183] The Jayamaṅgalā holds that the knowledge is derived through the authoritative statement and it is applied through inference to the object denoted.[184] Diṅnāga, as recorded by Uddyotakara, holds when one comes to know the similarity through hearing the authoritative statement, it becomes a case of verbal testimony.[185] According to Veṅkaṭanātha, the Upamāna is the authoritative statement. It is of three kinds as it conveys the elements of similarity dissimilarity and the descriptive qualities. The sentence conveying these, however, is not different from verbal testimony.[186]

Veṅkaṭanātha criticises the view of Udayana that through Upamāna we recognise the object denoted by the authoritative statement. Here, objects Veṅkatanātha, the knowledge of the denotative relation which forms the purpose of Upamāna is cognised through the authoritative statement itself.[187] Nor can it be proper to say with Udayana that the similarity is here the factor for restricting the use of a certain word to the certain object and it is not cognised through the authoritative statement. The similarity in general was cognised through the authoritative statement and becomes clear at the sight of the *gavaya*. If it is not admitted that the object is cognised in general, it would lead to the undesirable contingency of the non-arising of knowledge in case of the supra sensuous objects like Indra because the particular arrangement of the component parts which are the factors for restricting the words in a particular sense are not cognised in these cases.[188] It can in no way be denied that the general meaning is not apprehended in these cases.[189] Śrīnivasādāsa also states that Upamāna may very well be included under verbal testimony if the stress is laid upon the authoritative statement.[190] Diṅnāga, as quoted by Uddyotakara, favours the inclusion of Upamāna under verbal testimony as one of the alternatives. If one comes to know the similarity through hearing the authoritative statement, it becomes a case of verbal testimony.[191] Kumārilabhaṭṭa records the view of Vātsyāyana that Upamāna is the authoritative sentence itself. This is, however, included under the verbal testimony.[192] Here, the validity of meaning conveyed depends upon the knowledge of the speaker of the authoritative statement. It turns it into a case of verbal testimony only.

The Naiyāyikas spare no pain to prove the Upamāna as different from verbal testimony. The view of Diṅnāga, states Uddyotakara, is based upon misunderstanding of the purpose of Upamāna. Diṅnāga wrongly thinks that what is apprehended through Upamāna is either the resemblance to the cow or the existence of *gavaya* as qualified by the resemblance to the cow, Diṅnāga wrongly deduces such a meaning from the *sūtras* of Gautama. The purport of the statement of Gautama, however, is that one realises the denotative relation through the well known similarity.[193] Vācaspati tries to prove that Upamāna cannot be a case of verbal testimony. The verbal testimony cannot lead to the knowledge of denotative relation. It conveys that the object denoted is different from the object of its own class and those of other classes. That is why even after hearning the authoritative statement one is observed to be desirous of knowing the object denoted.[194] Moreover, the denotative relation cannot be comprehended without the perception of one of the relata to the genus. The *gavaya* unlike the sky, etc., (i.e., singular terms) is a general term which denotes many *gavayas*. Thus, the word like *gavaya* conveys the object through the knowledge of the genus of the object. Such a relative is not comprehended merely through the sentence conveying the similarity. The perception of *gavaya* is the source of knowing the genus of *gavaya* and the denotative relation between the word *gavaya* and the animal *gavaya* is conveyed through the authoritative statement. Therefore, authoritative statement alone cannot lead to the knowledge of the denotative relation.[195]

Jayantabhaṭṭa is aware of the objections against the view of Vātsyāyana and argues that Upamāna cannot be included under verbal testimony. The totality of cause is not the same in both the cases. The verbal testimony operates through the verbal understanding or the validity of the knowledge of the speaker. The Upamāna, however, requires the additional factor of other means, i.e., well known similarity. It would have very well been included under verbal testimony if the forest-dweller would not have instructed the city-dweller desirous of knowing the *gavaya* about similarity to the well known object which serves as a means of knowing the *gavaya*.[196] The case is analogous to the inference for other (*parataḥ anumāna*) where the knowledge is derived through a probans, but the words are inevitable to convey the sense.[197] Similarly, here also the knower knows the object through well known similarity and not merely through the words. The knower understands the well known similarity through the authoritative statement and knows thereby the denotative relation. Thus merely the authoritative statement does not lead to the knowledge acquired through Upamāna. It is the understanding of the well known similarity that the reliable person conveys which leads to the knowledge of the denotative relation.[198] Jayantabhaṭṭa is further aware of the fact that some systematists try to include Uddyotakara's view of Upamāna also under verbal testimony. Against such an attempt Jayantabhaṭṭa argues that Upamāna cannot be a case of Verbal testimony also. The knowledge of the denotative relation cannot be generated by the statement of the forest-dweller only for the *gavaya* is not present at the time of instruction given by the forest-dweller and the knowledge of such a relation is possible when both the name and its denotation are known and not otherwise.[199] The authoritative statement does not directly lead here to the knowledge of denotative relation because the object conveyed is not present at a time of hearing the statement. In the case of Upamāna, all the rational doubts about the contents of the knowledge are not satisfactorily answered at the time of hearing the statement. It depends upon perception for the completion of the expressed sense. Verbal testimony, however, carries with it a sense of completion and requires no other proof for the complete expression of its object.[200] It may be argued here that the authoritative statement conveys the denotative relation with the class and it is verified through the perception of the individual object. This will, however, not disprove the position of the Naiyāyikas since the class is not definitely known without perceiving an individual.[201] Moreover, if the knowledge is said to be derived through the verbal testimony, it would be a case of doubtful knowledge because we have no faith in the veracity of the statement.[202] Udayana further adds if the resultant knowledge through Upamāna is considered to be a case of verbal testimony, such a knowledge would be admitted as arising in a person who has heard the authoritative statement but has not perceived the *gavaya*.[203] Moreover, the similarity to the cow is not a cause of usage of the word *gavaya* in the sense of the animal *gavaya*.

Otherwise, the denotation of the word *gavaya* would not be known by the people who do not know the cow. Hence, the similarity conveyed through the authoritative statement does not serve as a cause to know the denotative relation between the word *gavaya* and the animal *gavaya*.[204]

Udayana further tries to prove that the Upamāna cannot be case of the combination of the perception and verbal testimony as well. In the case of Upmāna the perception of *gavaya* and the authoritative statement regarding the denotation take place at different times. The authoritative statement is heard earlier and the perception of the object takes place afterwards. However, the objects which produce the effect together should operate and should be present at the same time in producing the effect.[205] Nor should it be argued that the remembrance of the authoritative statement is still present at the time of perceiving the *gavaya*, thus they can be postulated as present at the same time and consequently Upamāna may be a case of the combination of perception and verbal testimony. The knowledge of similarity cannot be a result of perception for according to the Vaiśeṣikas, as in the case of the followers of Kumārilabhaṭṭa, the similarity is not a genus so that it may be perceived by the same organ which perceives an object. Thus, in the absence of knowledge of similarity such a remembrance is not effective.[206] Again, if it is argued that Upamāna is the combination of the result perception and verbal testimony, it would involve the undesirable contingency of inclusion of inference and verbal testimony also under perception because they are result of *liṅga parāmarśa* and the knowledge of the *pada* respectively which are in turn the result of perception.[207]

Upamāna versus recognition

The Jaina logicians and Meghanādasūri a follower of Viśiṣṭādvaita system include Upamāna under recognition. They hold that the purpose of Upamāna postulated by the Naiyāyikas, can be served by recognition. The process involves elements of more than one means of knowledge. Recognition found in the cases like 'this is the same pot' is based upon earlier cognition of the pot. Similarly, in the case of Upamāna also the object to by known is already cognised. In the stock example of the Naiyāyikas the knowledge of denotative relation is already cognised through the statement of the forest-dweller. There is, therefore, no factor to differentiate Upamāna from recognition.[208] Meghanādasūri quotes the view of Udayana and maintains that Upamāna envisaged by him is a case of recognition.[209] Otherwise, we have to postulate some additional means of knowledge in the case like 'this is the same Devadatta'[210] or the sense conveyed through the sentences like 'there are fruits on the bank of the river.'[211]

The Naiyāyikas, however, would not admit such a position for Upamāna. Firstly, the Jaina view presupposes the theory that the denotative relation was cognised through the assertion of the authoritative person. As stated in the Naiyāyikas' objection to the imclusion of Upamāna under verbal testimony, the Naiyāyikas do not admit that the denotative relation was already cognised through the verbal assertion. It is also wrong to say that the denotative relation is perceived later on. Secondly, the recognition cannot have the denotative relation as its object because the denotation of the words is beyond the senses. It cannot be argued further that the Naiyāyikas would have to accept some other *pramāṇa* for the cases like 'this is the same Devadatta', because the Naiyāyikas include such cases under perception itself. The other exasmple supplied by Meghanādasūri is a case of verbal testimony. Moreover, it would again be wrong from the Nyāya point of view to include Upamāna under recognition because it involves the element of two means of knowledge. Though it has the element of perception and verbal testimony, yet its independent nature cannot be denied because the resultant knowledge as a whole cannot be explained by two only.[212] Thus, it would not be plausible to include it under the recognition which according to the Jainas include any type of knowledge containing the elements of more than one means of knowledge.

Upamāna versus Remembrance

Śāntarakṣita suggests as an alternative that the Nyāya view of Upamāna can be included under remembrance. He argues that in the stock example of the Naiyāyikas the denotative relation is known at the time of hearing the authoritative statement and as such the Upamāna does not convey something new.[213] Here, the Naiyāyikas cannot argue that the name was not cognised earlier. Otherwise, no one would have the notion that this is the object the name of which was heard by him.[214] Śāntarakṣita further reiterates the view of Aviddhakaraṇa which is adopted by Udayana also that through the authoritative statement one knows the denotative relation of a word to the class and it is through Upamāna that the same is known with reference to a single object.[215] To this also Śāntarakṣita objects that it is incongruous to know the denotative relation with reference to one thing and to apply it to the other.[216] Śāntarakṣita further argues that the theory of the Naiyāyikas contains two things, viz., the name and its denotation. The name is known through communication of the convention by the authoritative person and the denotation is directly perceived because the denotation has no existence apart from the objects denoted. Thus there remains nothing to be cognised through Upamāna. The case is analogous to the knowledge of 'fragrant' and 'sweet.' There is, thus, nothing to defferentiate Upamāna from remembrance.[217]

The view of Śāntarakṣita is based upon the assumption that the denotative relation is known through the authoritative statement. This is, however, discussed in details in connection with Naiyāyikas, attempt to disprove the inclusion of Upamāna under verbal testimony and, hence, it would be needless to repeat the whole discussion here.

Here, it may also be obsesved that besides the arguments against the independent status of Upamāna, a set of arguments is directed against Upamāna as a mode of conveying the denotation. The critics suggest that uncommon attributes and the attributes in general should not be grouped with similarity firstly for such a notion goes against our common experience[218] and secondly because if the modes are taken to be the means of knowledge, it would imply as many *Pramāṇas* as the modes.[219] However, both the points have little force. It is also contradicted by our common experience that object is not known through a statement of dissimilarity or the description of common properties. The examples offered by Vācaspati and others explain the position beyond doubt. Nor does the position imply the acceptance of indefinite number of the *pramāṇas* because the analysis of the modes involved in Upamāna shows that there is no more mode of conveying the denotative relation involving Upamāna. It cannot be stated that all the other modes like grammar, dictionary, etc., conveying the denotative relation fall in the category of Upamāna because such a position is not accepted by any one. It can only be stated that the Upamāna is the mode of conveying the denotative relation. It is never state that all the modes of conveying denotative relation fall under Upamāna. Through Mokṣākaragupta does not admit such a relation, yet it does not present a serious problem. Some kind of relation between the word and the object denoted by it will have to be accepted, though it may not be given a particular name. Such a relation can be conveyed through Upamāna in some cases.

In this way, we can say with Bhāsarvajña that Upamāna is serviceable to verbal testimony. But, at the same time the view of including it under verbal testimony cannot be accpted because the Upamāna, unlike the verbal testimony, does not depend upon the statement only. It requires in addition the perception of the similarity for the complete expression of its object while in the case of verbal testimony the sense is completed at hearing the statement of the reliable person only. Nor can it be proper to say that the Upamāna is a case of remembrance for the remembrance is caused by the past impressions only while the Upamāna requires the perception of the object as well.

The criticism of the Nyāya concept of Upmāna found in the texts of the other systematists further reveals that most of the arguments of the opponents are centred around the absence of some object to be cognised merely through Upamāna. Kumārilabhaṭṭa and his followers contend that the result achived through Upamāna can be attained through the combination of the perception and the verbal testimony or by the verbal testimony assisted by perception. The argument can be alleviated by the Naiyāyikas on the basis of their theory of *pramāṇasamplava*. They hold that it is not a condition for a *pramāṇa* to cognise some object not cognised by some other source of knowledge. What determines the independent nature of *pramāṇa* is its totality of causal condition and the nature of resultant knowledge. When these are different from all other means of knowledge in the case of Upamāna, the Upamāna is considered as an independent source of knowledge. So through it is a combination of totality of causal conditions of perception and memory, it leads to the acceptance of independent means of knowledge.

As a matter of fact, the critics are right to say that the elements of Upamāna can be explained through one or the other means of knowledge. The observation of similarity which the perceptible object bears to the remembered one is a case of perception; the statement of the reliable person is a case of verbal testimony; the recollection of the meaning of the statement is a case of memory and the element of cogning an unknown object through the well known one is a case of inference. However here the critics ignore to examine the combined process which, of course, requires novelty in the activity of mind. The mental operation is distinct from that involved in the other means of knowledge. This, in turn, results into more than a single means of knowledge. This leads the Naiyāyikas to accept Upamāna as a distinct means of knowledge.

Footnotes :

1. N.S.1.1.1
2. प्रसिद्धसाधर्म्यात्साध्यसाधनमुपमानम् ।

   N.S. 1.1.6
3. N.S. 1.1.4
4. N.S. 1.1.7
5. अत्यन्तप्रायैकदेशसाधर्म्यादुपमानासिद्धिः.
6. प्रसिद्धसाधर्म्यादुपमानसिद्धेर्यथोक्तदोषानुपपत्तिः ।

   N.S. 2.1.46
7. N.V.2.1.45
8. प्रज्ञातेन सामान्यात्प्रज्ञापनीयस्य प्रज्ञापनमुपमानमिति ।

   N.V. 1.1.6
9. समाख्यासम्बन्धप्रतिपत्तिः उपमानार्थ इत्याह ।

   N.B. 1.1.7.
10. यथा गौरेवं गवय इत्युपमाने प्रयुक्ते ।

    N.B. 1.1.6
11. Here, it may be observed that Vātsyāyana refers to both—similarity and the authoritative statement as the means. In the process of attaining the knowledge, however, both of these are different. The authoritative sentence is heard first and the knowledge of similarity arises through remembering the statement and as such the latter comes to be the Vyāpāra.

12. N.B. 1.1.6
13. प्रसिद्धं साधर्म्यं यस्य, प्रसिद्धेन वा साधर्म्यं यस्य, सोऽयं प्रसिद्धसाधर्म्यो गवयः। तस्मात् साध्यसाधनमिति।

N.V. 1.1.6

14. समाख्यासम्बन्धप्रतिपत्तिरुपमानार्थः।

N.V.1.1.6

15. यदा ह्यनेन श्रुतं भवति यथा गौरेवं गवय इति, प्रसिद्धे गोगवयसाधर्म्ये पुनर्गवयसाधर्म्यं पश्यति प्रत्यक्षम्। ततस्तस्य भवत्ययं गवय इति समाख्यासम्बन्धप्रतिपत्तिः।

N.V.1.1.6

16. आगमाहितसंस्कारस्मृत्यपेक्षं सारूप्यज्ञानमुपमानम्।

N.V.1.1.6. and N.V.T.T. theroon

17. प्रसिद्धसाधर्म्यादित्यत्र प्रसिद्धिरुभयी श्रुतमयी प्रत्यक्षमयी च। श्रुतमयी यथा गौरेवं गवय इति। प्रत्यक्षमयी च गोसादृश्यविशिष्टोऽयमीदृशः पिण्ड इति। तत्र प्रत्यक्षमयी प्रसिद्धिरागमाहितस्मृत्यपेक्षा समाख्यासम्बन्धप्रतिपत्तिहेतुः।

N.V.1.1.6

18. प्रसिद्धसाधर्म्यस्य वैधर्म्यस्य चोपमानहेतुत्वादप्रतिषेधः।

N.V.2.1.45

19. अत्रापि यत इत्यध्याहार्यम्।

N.V.T.T.1.1.6

20. साध्यसाधनमित्युच्यमाने प्रत्यक्षादिसाधनेषु सुखदुःखसाधनेषु प्रसङ्गः। अत उक्तं प्रसिद्धसाधर्म्यादिति।

N.V.T.T.1.1.6

21. N.V.T.T.1.1.6
22. साधर्म्यग्रहणं च धर्ममात्रोपलक्षणमिति करसंज्ञाप्रतीतिफलमप्युपमानमेवेति नाव्याप्तिः।

N.V.T.T. 1.1.6.also

ननु यदोदीच्येन क्रमेलकं निन्दतोक्तम्, धिक्करभमतिदीर्घवक्रग्रीवं प्रलम्बोष्ठं कठोरतीक्ष्णकण्टकाशिनं कुत्सितावयवसन्निवेशमपसदं पशूनामिति, तदुपश्रुत्य दाक्षिणात्य उत्तरापथं गतस्तादृशं वस्तूपलभ्य नूनमसौ करभ इति प्रत्येति।

N.V.T.T. 1.1.6

23. अत एव बहून्युदाहरणान्युक्त्वाप्याह स्म भगवान् भाष्यकारः एवमन्योऽप्युपमानस्य लोके विषयो बुभुत्सितव्य इति।

N.V.T.T. 1.1.6

24. N.M. Part I, p. 128

25. N.M. Part I., p. 129

26. अत्रातिदेशवाक्यार्थस्त्रिविधः परिगृह्यते।
साधर्म्यं धर्ममात्रं च वैधर्म्यं चेति भेदतः॥

T.R., p.87

27. तत्र यथा गौस्तथा गवय इति श्रुतातिदेशवाक्यस्य पश्चाद् वनं गतस्य नागरिकस्य वाक्यानुभूतस्य गोसदृशस्य गवये यत् प्रतिसन्धानमयमसौ गोसदृश इति तत्साधर्म्योपमानम्।

N.Sa.S., T.R., p. 87

28. वैधर्म्योपमानं तु कीदृगश्व इति प्रश्ने गवादिद् द्विशफो न भवत्यश्व इत्यतिदेशवाक्याद्गवादिवैसादृश्यमधिगतवतः पश्चादेकशफत्वादिरूपस्य वैसादृश्यस्य तुरङ्गमे प्रत्यभिज्ञानम्।

N.Sa.S., T.R., p.87

29. वैधर्म्यविशिष्टपिण्डदर्शनं करणम्, जलादिविधर्मगुणवती पृथिवीत्यतिदेशवाक्यार्थस्मृतिव्यापारः।

Dinakarī, p. 263
also cf. N.Si. M., p. 127

30. N.Sa.S., T.R., p. 88

31. एवं गन्धवती पृथिवीत्युत्तरेऽपि ज्ञेयम्।

N.S.M., p. 127.

32. गवा गवयसारूप्यं प्रतिपद्यते गवयसत्तां वेत्यहो प्रमाणाभिज्ञता भदन्तस्य।

N.V.1.1.6. and

तदीदृशमुपमानफलमविद्वान् सादृश्यविशिष्टवस्तुज्ञानं चोपमानफलमिति भ्रान्तो भदन्तो दिग्नागः।

N.V.T.T.1.1.6.

33. Fragments from Dinnāga, p. 50-51.

34. N.B. 1.1.6.

35. N.M. part I, P. 132

36. प्रमाणशास्त्रत्वादस्य प्रमाणमेवार्थपरिच्छित्तिसाधनमिहोपदिश्यते प्रमेयं तु मोक्षाङ्गमेवोपदिश्यते इत्यलं प्रसङ्गेन।

N.M., Part I, p. 132.

37. अत्यन्तप्रायैकदेशसाधर्म्यादुपमानासिद्धिः।

N.S. 2.1.45.

38. प्रसिद्धसाधर्म्यादुपमानसिद्धेर्यथोक्तदोषानुपपत्तेः।

N.S. 2.1.46.

39. N.V. 2.1.46.
40. N.S. 2.1.47-49.
41. प्रत्यक्षो गवयस्तावत् सादृश्यस्मृतिस्त्र तु ।

S.V., up. 7.

42. ननु सादृश्ययुक्तेऽर्थे न स्मृतिर्नेन्द्रियाद् गतिः ।

S.V., up.7

43. पूर्वावाक्यार्थविज्ञानान्नाधिक्यं गवये यदि ।
स्मरणादविशिष्टत्वात् सङ्गतेर्न प्रमाणता ॥

S.V., up. 8.

44. अथ त्वधिकता काचित् प्रत्यक्षादिवशाद् भवेत् ।
यावद्धीन्द्रियसम्बन्धे तत्प्रत्यक्षमिति स्मृतम् ॥

S.V.,up., 9.

45. स्मर्यमाणस्य चांशस्य विवेकेनाप्रमाणता ।

S.V., up, 10.

46. N.R., up. 10.
47. श्रुतातिदेशवाक्यत्वं न चातीवोपयुपज्यते ।
येऽपि ह्यश्रुततद्वाक्यास्तेषामपि भवत्ययम् ।
प्रत्यक्षदृष्टगोत्वानां वने गवयदर्शिनाम् ॥

S.V., up. 10-11

48. न च शब्दार्थसम्बन्धः प्रमेयोऽत्र तदेष्यते ।
सादृश्यावधृते वाक्ये वाक्यादवगतो ह्यसौ ॥

S.V., up. 13

49. न चास्य प्रत्यभिज्ञानं पुनरुत्पद्यते वने ।
शक्त्योरतीन्द्रियत्वेन स्मृतिरेव हि सेष्यते ।

S.V., up. 14

50. स्यादेवं यदि शक्तौ देशकालाधिक्यं स्यात्र तु तदस्ति, ततोऽनधिकार्श्रत्वात् शक्तिज्ञानं स्मृतिरेव ।

N.R., up. 14

51. शब्दानुविद्धबोधेऽपि प्रत्यक्षमुपपादितम् ।

S.V., up. 15

52. यदिदं दुर्मतं हेयं यतः सम्बन्धधीरियम् ।
प्रत्यक्षानुगृहीतेन शाब्देनैवोपजन्यते ॥

M.M., p. 115

53. M.M., p. 116

54. उपमानपदं लोके सादृश्ये सति विश्रुतम् ।
वैधर्म्ये धर्ममात्रे च तत्प्रयोगः कथं हि वः ॥
तथातिदेशशब्दोऽपि वाक्ये साधर्म्यबोधके ।
प्रसिद्धः सोऽपि चान्यत्र कथ्यमानो दुनोति माम् ॥
M.M., p. 116
55. P.P., p. 271
56. N.C., p. 290
57. N.C., p. 290
58. त्रिविधमप्यतिदेशवाक्यागम एव ।
N.P., p. 491
59. तदप्यनुपपन्नं प्रागेव व्युत्पत्तिसिद्धेः ।
N.P., p. 491
60. प्रथममेव वाक्यार्थतया प्रतीतेः गोसादृश्योपलक्षितः कश्चित्तत्त्वार्थविशेषो गवय इति हि प्रतीतिः। पश्चात् प्रत्यक्षितगवयस्य वैशद्यमात्रमेव ।
N.P., p. 491
61. एवं नित्यातीन्दियविषयसंस्काररामादिशब्दानामपि नित्यमव्युत्पत्तिरेव ।
N.P., p. 491-2
62. तत्र, गवयगवयशब्दयोः सम्बन्धिधियः प्रत्यभिज्ञाप्रत्यक्षत्वात् ।
N.D.M., p. 215
63. प्रमाणान्तरे च सोऽयं देवदत्तः इत्यादावपि तथात्वम् ।
N.D.M., p. 215
64. न च 'अस्य गवयशब्दसंज्ञा' इति धीरुपमानम्, तस्य वनेचरवाक्यादवगतत्वेन स्मृतित्वात् ।
N.D.M., p. 215
65. सादृश्यं चानेकम् । तच्च सदृशानेकावयवजम् ।
N.D.M., p. 215
66. व्याप्तिग्रहणापेक्षात्वादनुमानेऽन्तर्भावः ।
Y.M.D., p. 35
67. स्मरणरूपत्वात्तस्य प्रत्यक्षेऽन्तर्भावः ।
Y.M.D., p. 35
68. वाक्यजन्यत्वात् शब्दे वा अनर्भावः ।
Y.M.D., p. 35
69. तदेतत् त्रयमप्यनुमान एवान्तर्भूतम् ।
Jay. On P.P., p. 46

70. यथा खल्वन्वयिनो व्यतिरेकिणश्च प्रयोगप्रकारवैचित्र्येऽपि नानुमानाद्बहिर्भावः अनुमान-विशेषत्वात्।

Jay. On P.P., p. 46

71. अपेक्षितसाधर्म्यसद्भावाच्च तथाऽत्रारीति।

Jay. On P.P., p.46

72. P.R.K., p. 148

73. अन्यथा योग्यानुपलब्धेरपि मानान्तरत्वापत्तेः।

P.R.K., p. 148

74. P.R.K., p.148

75. ibid

76. तदुत्तरमेतत्पदवाच्यत्वेनैवं जानामीत्यनुव्यवसायेन मानसत्वनिश्चयाच्चेति।

P.R.K., p. 148

77. उपमानस्य दृष्टान्तमात्रैकविग्रहत्वेनानुमानावयव उदाहरणेऽन्तर्भावः।

P.P.G.V., p. 244

78. N. V.I.I. 6

79. तथा परिगृहीतार्थग्रहणान्न प्रमाणता।
स्मृतिरेवोपमानस्य करणार्थवियोगतः॥

T.S., 1564

80. अनन्तोपायजन्याश्च समाख्यायोगसंविदः।

T.S., 1580

81. यतः प्रमाण्यं नाम विषयवत्तया व्याप्तम्। न चास्य निपुणमपि निरूपयन्तो विषयं पश्यामः।

B.T.B., p. 6

82. तथा हि समाख्यासम्बन्धस्तस्य विषयो वर्ण्यते। स च परमार्थतो नास्ति।

B.T.B., p. 6

83. उपमानं प्रसिद्धसाधर्म्यात् साध्यसाधनम्। तद्वैधर्म्यात् प्रमाणं किं स्यात् संज्ञाप्रतिपादनम्।

Laghiyastraya 3.10. Quoted by Hemacandra in Pramāṇamimaṁsā, p. 30.

84. इदमल्पं महद् दूरमासन्नं प्रांशु नेति वा।
व्यपेक्षातः समर्थेऽर्थे विकल्पः साधनान्तरम्॥

Laghīyastraya 3.12, Quoted by Hemacandra in Pramāṇa-mīmāsā, p. 39

85. साधर्म्याऽव्यतिरेकः उपायभूतत्वात्।

Y.D., p. 32

86. आख्यातृप्रामाण्यादेव प्रतिपत्तुर्गवयविज्ञानमुत्पद्यते ।

Y.D., p. 32

87. अथैवंजातीयकानामपि प्रमाणान्तरत्वमिष्यते तेनात्यल्पमिदमुच्यते चत्वारि प्रमाणानीति । किं तर्हि पाणिविहाराक्षिनिकोचप्रभृतीनामप्युपसंख्यानं कर्त्तव्यम् ।

Y.D., p. 32

88. उपमानं तावद्यथा गौस्तथा गवय इति वाक्यं तज्जनिता धीरागम एव। योप्ययं गवयशब्दो गोसादृश्यस्य वाचक इति प्रत्ययः सोऽप्यनुमानमेव।

S.T.K., 5

89. आप्तेनाप्रसिद्धगवयस्य गवा गवयप्रतिपादनादुपमानमाप्तवचनमेव ।

P.B., p. 214

90. तेषामपि यथा गौर्गवयस्तथेति वाक्यं तज्जनिता च बुद्धिरागम एव। यदपि गोसदृशस्य गवयशब्दवाच्यत्वज्ञानं तदप्यनुमानम्, तत्र तच्छब्दप्रयोगात् ।

N.K., p. 533

91. Vaiśeṣikasūtropaskāra 3, p. 508
92. गोपिण्डान्तरेऽपि संकेतग्रहणे प्रमाणान्तराभिधानप्रसङ्ग इति ।

N. Sāra, p. 73

93. N. Sāra, p. 73
94. शब्दप्रामाण्यसमर्थनं प्रयोजनम् ।

N. Sāra, p. 75

95. परीक्षा त्वर्थापत्तिवत्प्रमाणस्य सतः प्रमाणेष्वन्तर्भावविज्ञापनार्थमिति ।

N.Sāra, p. 76

96. अन्तर्भावस्त्वनुमान एवास्य यथाश्रुतोऽपि निराकृतो नागम इति ।

N.Sāra, p. 76

97. अस्य सूत्रकारस्यैवंस्वभावत्वाद्यत्सिद्धान्तमपि क्वचिन्नाभिधत्ते। यथा कृत्स्नैक-देशविकल्पादिनावयविनिराकरणे ।

N.Sāra, p. 77

98. N. Sāra, p. 76
99. 'यथा गौस्तथा गवयं' इति आप्तवचनमेवातिदेशवाक्यमेवोपमानं प्रमाणमित्यर्थः। वाक्यादेव सञ्ज्ञासञ्ज्ञिसम्बन्ध परिच्छेदस्यापि सिद्धेः।

Kiraṇāvalī, p. 215

100. N.K., p. 530-31
101. N.K., p. 533-34
102. Y.D., 4
103. S.T.K., 5

104. G.B., 4
105. Jay., 4
106. Jay., 4
107. M.V.4
108. S.C., 4
109. उपमानैतिह्यादीनां चानुमानशब्दयोः प्रवेशः ।

S.P.B., 1.88

110. N.V.1.1.6 and N.V.T.T. Thereon.
111. S.T., 15.64
112. T.S., 1574-5
113. ibid
114. त्रिविधमप्यतिदेशवाक्यागम एव ।

N.P., p. 491

115. गवयगवयशब्दयोः सम्बन्ध धियः प्रत्यभिज्ञाप्रत्यक्षत्वात् ।
116. Y.M.D., p. 34-35
117. Jay. On P.P., p. 46
118. P.R.K., p. 148
119. यावद्धीन्द्रियसम्बद्धं तत्प्रत्यक्षमिति स्मृतम् ।

S.V., up. 9

120. स्मर्यमाणस्य चांशस्य विवेकेनाप्रमाणता ।

S.V., up. 10
also N.R. thereon.

121. प्रत्यक्षे गवये सादृश्यज्ञानं प्रत्यक्षफलम् ।

N.K., p. 534

122. स्मरणरूपत्वात् तस्य प्रत्यक्षेऽन्तर्भावः ।

Y.M.D., p. 34-35

123. सादृश्यातिदेशवाक्यार्थस्मरणसहकारेण चक्षुरादिनैव संज्ञासंज्ञिपरिच्छेदोपपत्तौ सादृश्यज्ञानादेर्मानान्तरत्वकल्पनस्यायुक्तत्वात् ।

P.R.K., p. 148

124. अन्यथा योग्यानुपलब्धेरपि मानान्तरत्वापत्तेः ।

P.R.K., P. 148

125. न चैवं सत्युपमितेः सत्युपमितेः परोक्षत्वं व्याहन्येतेति वाच्यम् । इष्टापत्तेः ।

P.R.K., p. 148

126. P.R.K., p. 148

127 ibid

128. तदुत्तरमेतत्पदवाच्यत्वेनैनं जानामीत्यनुव्यवसायेन मनसा मानसत्वनिश्चयाच्चेति ।

P.R.K., p. 148

129. N.V. 1.1.6 and N.V.T.T. thereon.

130. N.V. 1.1.6

131. तद्धीन्द्रियजनितमपि धूमज्ञानमिव तदगोचरप्रमेयप्रमितिसाधनात्प्रमाणान्तरम् ।

N.M. Part I, p. 129

132. प्रत्यक्षं तावदेवैतद्विषये न कृतश्रमम् । वनस्थगवयाकारपरिच्छेदफलं हि तत् ।

N.M. Part I, p. 129

133. नापि प्रत्यक्षफलम् अश्रुतवाक्यस्यापि प्रसङ्गात् ।

N.Ku. p. 334

134. P.B., p. 530-1. and N.K. threreon.

135. N.K., p. 534

136. Vaiśeṣikasūtropaskāra, p. 507

137. अतिदेशवाक्यश्रवणसमये गवयत्वं प्रवृत्तिनिमित्तं न ज्ञातमतः कथं संज्ञापरिच्छेद इति चेत् लक्षणया तत्प्रतीतिसम्भवात् ।

Vaiśeṣikasūtropaskāra p. 507

138. P.Pan., p. 271

139. S.T.K., 5

140. N.C., p. 290

141. M.V., 4

142. S.P.B., I.88

143. S.C., 4

144. Jayam. 4

145. Jay. On P. Pra., p. 46

146. Rāghavendraṭikā on Jaya. On P. Pra, p. 47
and Śrinivāsatīrtha's commentary thereon

147. अत्रोपमानद्वयस्यान्तर्भावानुक्तिः अतिस्फुटप्रतिभासत्वात्...... ।

Jay. On P.Pra., p. 46

148. Rāghavendraṭīkā on Jay. On P. Pra., p. 47

149. Jay. On P. Pra., p. 46

150. T.S. 1574-75

151. Pañcikā on T.S. 1575

152. बुद्धिस्थो न चेत् तस्यामवस्थायां भवेदसौ। क्रियते समयः कस्मिन्नयं च सदृशो गवा॥

T.S. 1576

153. प्रत्यक्षेणाप्रत्यक्षसिद्धेः।

N.S. 2.1.48

154. Ibid

155. N.S. 2.1.48

156. तथेत्युपसंहारादुपमानसिद्धेर्नाविशेषः।

N.S. 2.1.49

157. N.B. 2. 1.48

158. परार्थं चोपमानम्, यस्य ह्युपमेयमप्रसिद्धं तदर्थं प्रसिद्धोभयेन क्रियते इति ।

N.B.2.1.48

159. N.V.T.T., p. 358

160. N.M.Part I, p. 131

161. अस्त्वनुमानम्। तथाहि—गवयशब्दो गवयस्य वाचकः। असति वृत्त्यन्तरेऽभियुक्तैस्तत्र प्रयुज्यमानत्वात्, गवि गोशब्दवदिति

162......न। असिद्धेः न ह्यसति वृत्त्यन्तरे तद्विषयतया प्रयोगः सङ्गतिमविज्ञाय ज्ञातुं शक्यते।

N.Ku., p. 347

164. N,Ku., p. 349

165. N. Ku., p. 349

166. तथा च तद्योगप्राथम्याभ्यां तस्यैव व्याप्यत्वम्, ततः किं तेन? प्रकृतानुपयोगात्।

N.Ku., p. 349

167. किंलक्षणोऽसाविति प्रश्नार्थः।

N.Ku., p. 350

168. तदा व्यतिरेकपरं स्यात्, लक्षणस्य तथाभावात्।

N.Ku., 350-1

169. न ह्यनेन लिङ्गमविज्ञाय गवयशब्दस्य वाचकत्वं कस्यचिद्वाच्यत्वं नावगतं येन तदर्थं प्रश्नः स्यात्।

N.Ku., p. 352

170. नाऽनुमिनोमि न शृणोमि न स्मरामि किन्तूमिनोमीति प्रतीतेरपि प्रमित्यन्तरमेवोपमितिरिति भावः।

Rāmarudrī on N.S. Mu,

171. गोपिण्डान्तरेऽपि सङ्केतग्रहणे प्रमाणान्तराभिधानप्रसङ्ग इति ।

N.Sār., p. 73

172. शब्दप्रमाणसमर्थनार्थं प्रयोजनम् ।

N.Sār., p. 75

173. आप्तेनाप्रसिद्धगवयस्य गवयस्य गवा गवयप्रतिपादनादुपमानमाप्तवचनमेव ।

P.B., Kiraṇāvali., p. 214

174. तेषामपि यथा गौर्गवयस्तथेति वाक्यं तज्जनिता च लोके यः खलु गवय इति श्रुयते स गोसदृशः बुद्धिरागम एव ।

N.K., p. 533

175. Kiraṇāvalī, p. 215.

176. Y.D., 4

177. साधर्म्याऽव्यतिरेकः,उपायभूतत्वात्

Y.D., 4

178. Y.D., 4

179. अस्ति चोपमाने वक्तृविशेषापेक्षा ।

Y.D., 4

180. Y.D., 4

181. Y.D., 4

182. S.T.K., 5

183. G. on S.K., 4

184. Jayam, On S.K., 4

185. N.V.I.I. 6 and N.V.T.T thereon

186. त्रिविधमप्यतिदेशवाक्यागम एव ।

N.P., p. 491

187. तदप्यनुपपन्नं प्रागेव व्युत्पत्तिसिद्धेः ।

N.P., p. 491

188. एवं चानभ्युपगमे कथमिन्द्रादिशब्दव्युत्पत्तिः नह्यत्र निमित्तभूतसेस्थानविशेषादिदृष्टिः ।

N.P., p.491

199. N.P., p.491-2

190. वाक्यजन्यत्वात् शब्दे वा अन्तर्भाव ऊह्यः ।

Y.M.D., 35

191. N.V.I.I.6. and N.V.T.T. thereon.

192. S.V. up. 1-2

193. N.V. I. I. 6 and N.V.T.T:thereon

194. N.V.T : T. I. I. 6.

195. N. V. T. T. I.I.6
196. N.M. Part I, p. 129
197. उपायमात्रावगमे तु शब्दव्यापारो यथा परार्थानुमाने ।

N.M.Part I, p. 128-9

198. प्रतिपत्ताऽपि नागरको नारण्यवाक्यादेव तं प्राणिनं गवयशब्दवाच्यतया बुध्यते किं तु सारूप्यं प्रसिद्धेन गवा तस्य पश्यति........ ।

N.M. Part I, p. 129

199. आगमादपि तत्सिद्धिर्न वनेचरभाषितात् । तत्कालं संज्ञिनो नास्ति गवयस्य हि दर्शनम् । संज्ञासंज्ञिनोश्च परिच्छेदे सति तत्सम्बन्धः सुशको भवति नान्यथा... ।

N.M.Part I, p. 129

200. M.M. Part 1, p. 130
201. सम्बन्धप्रतिपत्तिश्च सामान्ये यदि नेष्यते ।
तदप्यविदितव्यक्ति न सम्यगवधारितम् ॥

N.M.Part I, p. 130

202. गवयाकारवृत्तिश्च तदानीं बुद्धद्युप प्लवः । सम्बन्धेऽपि द्व्यधिष्ठाने दधाति श्यामलां धियम् ।

N.M., Part I, P. 130

203. सेयं न तावद् वाक्यमात्रफलम् अनुपलब्धपिण्डस्यापि प्रसङ्गात् ।

N. Ku., p. 33

204. न हि गवयशब्दस्य सादृश्यं प्रवृत्तिनिमित्तम् अप्रतीतगूनामव्यवहारप्रसङ्गात् ।

N.Ku., p. 341

205. N.Ku., p. 334
206. वाक्यतदर्थयोःस्मृतिद्वारोपनीतावपि गवयपिण्डसम्बन्धेनापीन्द्रियेण तद्गतसादृश्यानुपलम्भे समयपरिच्छेदासिद्धेः ।

N.Ku., p. 335

207. फलसमाहारे तु तदन्तर्भावे अनुमानादेरपि प्रत्यक्षत्वप्रसङ्गात् ।

N.Ku., p. 336

208. एकत्वसादृश्यप्रतीत्योः सङ्कलनज्ञानरूपतया प्रत्यभिज्ञानतानतिक्रमात् ।

P.K.M., p. 345

209. गवयगवयशब्दयोः सम्बन्धधियः प्रत्यभिज्ञाप्रत्यक्षत्वात् ।

N.D.M., p. 215

210. प्रमाणान्तरवे च 'सोऽयं देवदत्तः' इत्यादावपि तथात्वम् ।

N.D.M., p. 215

211. किंच 'नद्यास्तीरे फलानि' इत्यादिवाक्यगतविषयप्रत्यक्षस्यापि प्रमाणान्तरत्वम्।

N.D.M., p. 215

212. Nyāya theory of Knowledge, p. 305
213. T.S. 1564
214. T.S. 1566
215. T.S. 1568
216. T.S. 1569-70
217. T.S. 1577-79
218. उपमानपदं लोके सादृश्ये सति विश्रुतम्। वैधर्म्ये धर्ममात्रे च तत्प्रयोगः कथं हि वः।

M.M., p. 116

219. अनन्तोपायजन्याश्च समाख्यायोगसंविदः।

T.S. 1580

CHAPTER 3

PŪRVAMĪMĀṀSĀ CONCEPT OF UPAMĀNA

The Pūrvamīmāṁsakas believe in Upamāna as an independent means of knowledge. Jaimini the authour of the *Mīmāṁsāsūtras* does not speak of Upamāna. It is Śabara who discusses the nature of Upamāna. The exposition of Śabara is commented on by both—Prabhākara and Kumārila the exponents of two different schools of Mīmāṁsā. There is, however, no fundamental difference regarding Upamāna in the view of the two Ācāryas. There is only a minor difference,viz., that Prabhākara considers similarity to be an independent category, while according to Kumārila it is the assemblage of common features. In our present discussion, therefore, we shall take up both the schools together.

Defining Upamāna Śabara says that Upamāna is the similarity which brings about the cognition of an object not in contact with the senses.[1] Śabara uses the same term for the means of knowledge and the resultant knowledge. In case of perception, inference, verbal testimony and implication Śabara defines the resultant knowledge. In the present case, however, he defines Upamāna in terms of the means of knowledge. The definition, however, leaves the nature of resultant knowledge unexplained. Śabara has expressed it with the help of an example 'just as the perception of the *gavaya* is the cause of the rememberance of the cow.'[2] In the definition the means of Upamiti is similarity but in the example it is 'the perception of the *gavaya.*' To avoid this absurdity the *gavayadarśana* should be understood in the sense of perception of the *gavaya* qualified by the similarity to the cow. In this way, we can understand similarity as leading to the memory of the cow.

As regards the resultant knowledge Śabara says that the result of Upamāna is the cognition of the object not in contact with the senses. He illustrates it as the remembrance of a cow. Here, the object of remembrance is, no doubt, not in contact with the senses but it leads to the undesirable contingency of the non-difference of Upamāna from remembrance. Kumārilabhaṭṭa also rejects this interpretation of Śabara on the ground that it would amount to remembrance.[3] Śālikanātha also criticises Śabara for using the word *smaraṇa* (remembrance). It is absurd to say that there arises knowledge of remembrance.[4] Here, it will not be worthwhile to assume that Śabara was not aware of the difficulty stated above. Hence, the interpretation involving the aforesaid difficulty is not tenable even from the view-point of Śabara. Therefore, the interpretation of the word gosmaraṇa requires further consideration.

To solve the above difficulty, *G.P. Bhatt* resorts to a new explanation of the term according to which the term *smaraṇa* does not mean an exact reproduction of a past cognition. On the other hand, Śabara uses the term *smaraṇa* in the sense of a cognition which is partly memory and partly fresh experience. He cites the case of the word *smaraṇa* in *gatismaraṇa* used by Śabara as an example of *sāmānyatodṛṣṭa anumāna.*[5] This solution is, however, not satisfactory, firstly for *G.P.Bhatt* himself fails to ascertain the element of experience in the present case and secondly it is difficult to establish that the term *smaraṇa* involves some new elements of experience. Here, it may be proposed that as the *gavayadarśana* is understood in the sense of the perception of *gavaya* qualified by its similarity, the term *gosmaraṇa* should also be taken in the sense of the remembrance of the cow as qualilfied by its similarity to the *gavaya* and the remembrance of this sort of object is the result of Upamāna.

Kumārilabhaṭṭa states that the object of Upamāna is the cognition of a thing remembered as quailfied by its similarity to the perceived object or the similarity as qualified by the previously known object.[6] A person who has seen the cow but has never seen the *gavaya* goes to the forest and happens to see a *gavaya* there. He cognises through the perception of *gavaya* its similarity to the cow. Then, he recalls to his mind the formerly perceived cow as similar to the *gavaya* perceived at that time. The cow which is remembered and is presently known as qualified by its similarity to the *gavaya* is the object known through Upamāna. Kumārilabhaṭṭa gives another alternate object of Upamāna as the similarity qualified by the previously known object.[7]

Pārthasārathi does not essentially differ from Kumārilabhaṭṭa. He defines Upamāna in terms of the resultant knowledge as the knowledge of similarity of the recollected object of past perception to present object as the cow perceived in the city is similar to *gavaya*.[8] Nārāyaṇa defines Upamiti and clarifies the notion of instrumentality and the resultant knowledge of Upamāna in clear terms. The knowledge of similarity which the *gavaya* bears is the means and the knowledge of similarity which the cow bears is the resultant knowledge.[9]

Prabhākara also understands similarity as the means of Upamāna. He takes with Śabara the perception of the *gavaya* as a means and the knowledge of some object not connected with the senses as the resultant knowledge. From the example offered by Śabara, the resultant knowledge seems to be in the form of remembrance of cow (*gosmaraṇa*). Prabhākara, however, construes the term *gosmaraṇa* in the sense of the agent in Upamāna and renders it as in the case of perception of one who has already seen a cow.[10] There remains nothing, in this case, to correspond to the resultant knowledge, viz., the object not connected with the senses. Thus, the nature of resultant knowledge, remains unexplained. From its explanation offered by Śālikanātha it seems that the resultant knowledge according to Prabhākara, is the knowledge of the cow. Here, cow should be taken as qualified by its similarity to the *gavaya*. To justify the above interpretation of the term *gosmaraṇa* Śalikanātha states that it cannot be interpreted in the sense of the resultant knowledge because there would arise no knowledge of remembrance of cow.[11] Śālikanātha defines Upamāna in terms of knowledge arising from the perception of similarity and having silmilarity as its object.[12] It is exemplified as the knowledge of similarity in the cow to the *gavaya* by perceiving the *gavaya* in the case of the person who has seen the cow.[13] Śālikanātha shows the significance of the words used by him in the definition. The expression *Sādṛśyāt dṛśyamānāt* (arising through the perception of similarity) excludes the knowledge of similarity arising from the sense-object contact.[14] The term *sādṛśyaviṣayaṁ jñānam* (the knowledge regarding similarity) excludes remembrance from the domain of Upamāna. Thus, it also excludes the knowledge of similarity arising through the authoritative statement from Upamāna because it is simply a case of remembrance.[15] The word *sādṛśya* also implies that the erroneous knowledge arising from apparent similarity *(sādṛśyābhāsa)* also is not included in Upamāna because it does not arise from *sādṛśya* proper and secondly there the discussion is about the valid knowledge and this kind of knowledge does not fall under this category.[16]

Kumārilabhaṭṭa mentions the practical utility of Upamāna as follows. It helps us to get the knowledge of the sacrificial details in case of a rite of which the details are not mentioned but are to be taken from some other rite. The sacrificial details, viz., the properties and appurteances not given in the *saurya* sacrifice are known as the same as mentioned in case of *āgneya* through Upamāna since both of these have the common deity.[17] Similarly, when the *vrīhis* kept for sacrifice are spoilt or stolen, *nivāra* can be used as a substitute of *vrīhi* with a view that the fruit will be the same. This is because the *nīvāra* is similar to the *vrīhi*.[18]

Similarity, according to Kumārilabhaṭṭa, must be some positive entity. There is no reason to negate the similarity as a positive entity. He defines similarity as the presence in one class of objects, of such an arrangement of the constituent parts as in common to other class of objects.[19] Here, clarifies Pārthasārathimiśra, the term constituent parts is the representative of both quality and activity. The term 'class of objects' denotes nothing but the other objects. What Kumārila means to say here is that similarity is the presence of properties in the constituent parts, qualities and activities in the same way as they are present in some other objects.[20] The more or less quantity in similarity depends upon the quantity of common properties.[21] Kumārilabhaṭṭa explains his position with the following illustration. The similarity between the lotus leaf and the eye lies in the fact that the parts of one are similar to those of other.[22] This proves that the similarity, according to Kumārilabhaṭṭa, lies in the parts of the object. The similarity seems to be of different kinds as it rests upon birth, property, substance, action power and the specific character. Sometimes, one of these may be common while sometimes more of these are common.[23] Pārthasārathi illustrates them as follows. Similarity of birth is found in the case of the fire and the *brāhmaṇa*, for both of them have their origin in prajāpati's mouth. Similarity of properties can be observed in case of two pictures. Similarity of substance is observed in case of two persons possessing similar wealth. Similarity of action is observed between the kite bird and the *śyena* sacrifice. Similarity of power is illustrated as that found between lion and Devadatta. Similarity of specific action is found between the second *prayāja* offering and the *pañcāvathanārāśaṁsa.* The similarity is an inherent relation and does not rest on their properties but in thier locus.[25] Hence, the properties themselves do not constitute similarity. It is not necessary for similarity to belong to many only. Sometimes it belongs to many and sometimes to a few only. That is why, we recognise similarity in twins though it belongs to two only.[26] The similarity is neither absolutely eternal nor subjected to utter annihilation. The similarity inheres in innumerable substrata and the destruction of any of these substrata implies its destruction in that only. No class is, however, subjected to utter destruction because it will have its substratum in some other individual.[27] The similarity is different from class also. In case we remember a class as belonging to the principal objects themselves, we have the idea of class but when the principal classes differ together we have an idea of similarity. Thus, the cow and the *gavaya* belong to different classes but are similar to each other. The similarity is, thus, an object of sense-pereception.[28]

Prabhākara tries to establish that similarity (*sādṛśya*) is a distinct entity.[29] Thus is further explained by Śālikanātha. He quotes the opinion of the Vaiśeṣikas as the opponent's stand and considers it from the view-point of the Prabhākara school. He quotes the opinion of the Vaiśeṣikas that either there is nothing called similarity different from substance, quality, action, generality, inherence and particularity or it is included in these categories only, because it is not enumerated in the list of the categories.[30] Śālikanātha criticises the view on the following grounds.

The existense of similarity is astablished through experience of similarity. The existence of a particular object is sought through its cognition. We find the congnition about similarity. Hence, its existence cannot be doubted.[31] Moreover, it cannot be included in any of the categories of the Vaiśeṣikas. The similarity cannot be a substance because it is found in case of the quality and action as well. It is neither quality nor action since it is found with reference to the quality and action also. It is not the cause of commonness. Hence, it is not generality also. Similarity cannot be included in inherence also because the latter is of the form of relation. The particluarity is not accepted even by the Naiyāyikas. So, there is no need of taking similarity as the form of particularity also. Hence, it should be accepted as a distinct entity.[32] The view of Prabhākara and his followers is criticised on the following grounds. The view cannot account for the cause of the differentiation into great and small degree in similarity. In the absence of degrees in similarity there would be no propriety for the cognition like 'the cow is very similar to *gavaya* but slightly similar to a boar'.[33] It cannot he held that the degree in smallness or greatness is caused by measurement or size, because there is no size in similarity. Size or measurement is found in case of the substance only. Nor can it be said that the difference in degree is caused by the size of the substratum of similarity because the substratum is the same in both the greater and smaller degree of similarity.[34] In the view of the Bhāṭṭas, however, this kind of ambiguity does not arise since the greater and the smaller degree in similarity depends upon the number of qualities, components and generality. When they are smaller in number the similarity is less and when they are larger in number, the similarity is more.[35]

Nārāyaṇa records here the view of Bhavanātha who defends the view of the Prābhākaras by pointing out the faults in the view of the Bhāṭṭas. If the similarity would mean merely the qualities, components and generality, the cognition should arise in the form of 'that.' However, as a matter of fact, the cognition aries in the form of 'similar to that.' Hence, similarity should be accepted as disinct entity.[36] The mere guess, says Nārāyaṇa, is not proper. The comprehension of the qualities, components and generality present in *gavaya* can take place in two ways: as existing in the cow and when considered in their own form. In the former case the resultant knowledge is in the form of 'similar to that' and in the latter case the resultant cognition is in the form of 'that'. Nārāyaṇa clarifies it with the following example. Devadatta when considered as born of Yajñadatta is cognised in the form 'son of Yajñadatta' and when considered in its own form is cognised as Devadatta.[37]

Udayana criticises the theory thus. The upholders of similarity as a distinct entity cannot explain the nature of similarity. If it is held to be a substratum not located anywhere else, it would be a substance. Again, if it is supposed to be revealed by some inseparable object, it would be a case of inherence. Its revelation will not be possible, if it is held to be revealed by some separable object. Moreover, in that case it would be of the nature of negation. Again, it would involve the impropriety of its revelation in the inseparable objects like the comoponents and the composite.[38] It can again be neither located in many nor in one. If it is held to be eternal and located in many, it would be a case of generality or class. There is no proof of support for the eternity of similarity. It cannot be considered to be eternal like generality. The generality is found located in so many objects and the destruction of one does not imply the absolute cessation of generality. This does not hold good in case of similarity. Hence, it cannot be considered to be eternal. If it is held to be located in a single object, it would not be eternal because if the location is destroyed, it would not be located anywhere. If again it is supposed to be eternal and located in a single object through identity, it would be a case of particularity.[39] If it is held to be possessed of existence (eternity), it would be a quality. Moerover, in that case it would not be possible to speak of similarity in case of non-eternal objects. If it is held to be a non-eternal object endowed with many similarities, it would again be a substance. If it is supposed to be without qualities, it would be a case of essence of qualities.[40] If it is supposed to be located in one object as a cause of conjunction and disjunction, it would be activity. If it is contrary to it, it would be a quality. Moreover, there would not arise the knowledge of similarity with reference to the qualities and the activities due to the similarity of their substratum, it would lead to the undesirable contingency of absence of the usage of similarity with refrence to the objects having dissimilar qualities and activities. Moreover, the supposition violates the rule of three kinds of cause.[41]

Mokṣākaragupta also argues that the similarity cannot be a distinct entity. If it is considered to be some distinct entity, it may be taken as an object of perception or otherwise. The former alternative does not hold good since it would imply the defect of non-perception of a perceptible object. The second alternative also involves the similarity of its non-estabishment because the similarity cannot be established through inference. There is no probans to prove the absurdity as a distinct category. Nor can it be proper to argue here that the similarity is establishel through the very notion of similarity because such a notion does not require similarity as a distinct category. The notion is produced from the very causes of similarity, viz., the objects said to be similar. Nor will it be right for the opponent to contend that similarity is established through Upamāna itself. The opponents themselves speculate that the relation of quilifier and qualificand which forms the object of Upamāna is found in the case of objects which are similar to each other. Hence, the application of Upamāna depends upon similarity and such a similarity cannot be established through Upamāna.[42]

The Mīmāṁsā theory of assigning an independent position to such a means of knowledge could not convince all the systematists. When such a means leads to the valid knowledge, it becomes a case of some other means of knowledge and as such it becomes a case of some other means of knowledge and as such it becomes needless to recognise it as independent means of knowledge. Broadly speaking, there are three elements in Upamāna postulated by the Mīmāṁasakas. For example, in the stock example of the Mīmāṁsakas firstly one has got the knowledge of the cow, secondly he perceives *gavaya* and thirdly there arises the final conclusion that the cow seen earlier is similar to this cow or the cow seen earlire bears these points of similarity. Here, the first two elements come under the mode of Upamāna and the last is the resultant knowledge. The critics of an independent status of Upamāna mainly take the element of resultant knowledge into consideration and hold that such a conclusion does not require some independent means of knowledge. They further find fault with the details of the modes and the resultant knowledge. The other systematists reject the independent status of the Upamāna on the following grounds.

The Mīmāṁsā view of the nature of resultant knowledge through Upamāna amounts to a case of memory. Consequently the resulant knowledge would not be valid.[43] Even on the basis of the practical utility of Upamāna postulated by the Mīmāṁaskas it need not be taken as a distinct source of knowledge. It would be a case of memory and as such it cannot bring out the efficacy of Upamāna. The Mīmāṁsakas hold that Upamāna helps to borrow the minor detials for a rite from another resembling to it. The purpose, however, is served by rememberance itself. The mention of the *Saurya* sacrifice, for example, reminds of the *Āgneya* sacrifice on account of similarity of the deity and the material offered.[44] If, for the sake of argument, it is conceded as differrent from memory, it may be included under inference. The knowledge arising of it can be deduced through syllogism.[45]

Udayana argues that there is no object to be known particularly through Upamāna. The Mīmāṁsakas hold that Upamāna is the means of cognising similarity. In that case, however, the knowledge of dissimilarity would also be a result of Upamāna.[46] Śrīdhara holds that the purpose of cognising similarity can be fulfilled by remembrance. The similarity is the conglomeration of common parts and this is cognised by perceiving the cow and is revived by perceiving the *gavaya*. Hence, it is a case of remembrance.[47] The Sāṁkhya also finds no purpose of postulation of Upamāna as a distinct means of knowledge. The similarity which is the object of Upamāna according to Mīmāṁsakas refers to that which the cow bears to the *gavaya*. It, however, is a case of perception since the similarity is the conglomeration of the parts and is observed in both the objects. It cannot be argued that the similarity which the directly perceived object, i.e., *gavaya* bears to the remembered object i.e., cow, is different from that found in cow and hence, the similarity which the object bears to the directly preceived one cannot be cognised at the sight of the directly perceived object.[48]

Śāntarakṣita also argues that there is no object which requires Upamāna for cognition. The Mīmāṁsakas hold that the Upamāna is required for cognizing the similarity which consists of the manifold of commonality of common parts. To this Śāntarakṣita replies that commonality being rejected, there arises no question of manifold commonality of component parts. Neither can it be regarded as a positive entity since commonality does not exist at all.[49] It is, therefore, inadimissible to accept it as a positive entity. Moreover, it would be a case of rememberance which is not a means of vaild knowledge at all.[50] On seeing a *gavaya* there arises the notion of its dissimilarity to the horse, etc. This would also be a distinct form of cognition.[51] If the nature of its being a distinct from of cognition is rejected on the ground that it is included ujder negation, the same holds good in the case of similarity. It can also equally be included under mutual negation.[52] In the case of dissimilarity, one cognises the negation of similarity and in case of similarity one cognises the negation of all common parts.[53] Thus, since the cognition relates to the presence of sereval similar parts, it would also fall under mutual negation. Otherwise if all the parts are considered to be similar, it would be a cause of identity which is not desirable.[54] If the Upamāna is regarded as distinct means of knowledge on the basis of such a slight element of validity, there would arise the undesirable contingency of accepting infinite number of means of knowledge because such a slight element of validity of knowledge is observed in various methods.[55] For example, when one sees a line of tress, after perceiving the second tree, one gets the idea that the earlier perceived one is first. This cognition would require a distinct means because it does not arise through dissimilarity or any other means postulated for rest of the kinds of cognitions.[56] If it is included under remembrance on the ground that it apprehends the tree already apprehended, the same may be the case with the object of Upamāna also.[57]

The Jainas also criticise the Mīmāṁsā position on the ground that Upamāna cannot be established as a distinct means of knowledge on the basis of comprehending similarity because it would involve other absurdities. The Mīmāṁsakas will be at a loss to explain the nature of means of comprehending dissimilaity. The Mīmāṁsakas will have to postulate some distinct means for cognising dissimilarity and it would go against the number of the means postulated by the Mīmāṁsakas.[58] The problem cannot be solved by taking dissimilarity as the negation of similarity because the similarity also can be taken as the negation of dissimilarity.[59]

The Viśiṣṭādvaitavādins also do not approve the indepedent status of Upamāna. Veṇkaṭanātha states that the Mīmāṁsā position would involve the undesirable contingency of admitting some additional means for knowing the dissimilarity which the remembered object bears to the direcly perceived one.[60] He further feels that the purpose of Upamāna can be served by either of the remembrance and inference.[61] The Dvaita, the Śuddhādvaita and the Dvaitādvaita schools of Uttaramīmāṁsā also do not approve the Mīmāṁsā view of admitting Upamāna as an indepedent means of knowledge mainly on the ground that the purpose of Upamāna can very well be served by the other means of knowledge.

As regards the inclusion of Upamāna under other means of knowledge, the views of other systematists can be summarised as follows. Bhāsarvajña includes it under remembrance[62] while Jayanta puts it under remembrance[63] or inference.[64] Udayana considers it a case of presumption and consequently favours its inclusion under inference.[65] Śrīdhara takes it as a case of remembrance.[66] Vācaspati in his *Śāṁkhyatattvakaumudi* includes it under perception.[67] According to Śāntarakṣita it is a case of remembrance.[68] The Jaina logicians favour its inclusion under *pratyabhijñā*.[69] Veṅkaṭanātha includes it in remembrance or inference[70] According to Jayatīrtha it is a case of any of perception, inference or verbal testimony.[71] Puruṣottama makes it a case of mental perception[72] and Mādhava Mukunda reduces it to either of perception or vaild testimony.[73] We proceed to discuss here the possibility of inlusion of Upamāna under any of the other means of knowledge.

Upamāna versus Perception

Vācaspati strongly favours the inclusion of Upamāna envisaged by the Mīmāṁsakas under perception. He lays emphasis on the fact that the similarity is the conglomeration of the parts common to two objects and such a conglomeration being identical in both the objects is perceived at the sight of the object of perception. He is aware of the Mīmāṁsā view that the similarity which forms the object of Upamāna pertains to the object which is not directly perceived but is remembered at the sight of a directly perceived object. Vācapati does not consider it over and above the knowledge arising of the sense-object contact because the object of perception is similar in both the cases.[74] The Mīmāṁsakas hold that the similarity is the conglomeration of the components of the body of one animal found to be almost the same in the body of another animal. The conglomeration being the same in both the cases is directly perceived at the sight of either of the two. Hence, it becomes a case of perception.[75] Jayatīrtha states when one acquires the knowledge of similarity which the directly perceived object bears to the earlier perceived one, it becomes a case of perception.[76] He does not explain the point any more. Puruṣottama considers it to be a case of mental perception. His argument is based upon the authority of perception of judgement *(anuvyavasāya)* which arises in the form that the object is congnised through mental perception.[77]

The Mīmāṁsakas, however, are not prepared to admit it a case of perception. Their main argument is that the object cognised here is not the similarity alone but the similarity as located in the object which is not in contact with the senses. Though the points of similarity are perceived yet the object qualified by the similarity is not directly perceived. The object is cognised through Upamāna and hence, it cannot be case of perception. Hence, Kumārilabhaṭṭa remarks that the object as qualified by similarity is not cognised by any other means and hence, it is the object of Upamāna only.[78] The Mīmāṁsakas further hold that the perception of the points of similarity in the directly perceived object is not the perception of the points of similarity which the remembered object bears to the former. These points of similarity cognised through Upamāna are located in an object which is not in contact with the senses and hence, it cases to be the object qualified by similarity, and it cannot be included under perception.

Upamāna versus Remembrance

Many systematists like Bhāsarvajña, Jayntabhṭṭa, Śrīdhara Śāntarakṣita and Veṅkaṭanātha try to reduce Upamāna to remembrance. Their main argument is this. The object of Upamāna, according to the Mīmāṁsakas, is the similarity which the remembered object bears to the object qualified by its similarity to the directly perceived one. The above systematists, however, hold that such an object was cognised earlier only and is remembered at the sight of the other object resembling to it. Hence, it becomes a case of remembrance and, thus, there remanis no need of postulating some additional means to cognise it. They are aware of the fact that the other correlative of similarity was not cognised earlier and as such the similarity as related to it was also not an object of cognition earlier. These authors solve the difficulty in their own way.

Bhāsarvajña states that the perception of the cow, in the stock example of the Mīmāṁsakas, involves the perception of its similarity to some other animal also because the similarity being inherent in it is perceived at the sight of the cow itself.[79] To overcome the above difficulty of the non-perception of the other correlative of similarity earlier, Bhāsarvajña holds when one saw the cow, he had the abstract (*nirvikalpa*) knowledge of similarity while the perception of the *gavaya* turns it into determinate (*savikalpa*). Thus, the perception of the *gavaya* revives the similarity already received and, hence, it becomes a case of remembrance, It is experienced in our common life also that the indeterminate (*nirvikalpa*) knowledge acquired earlier turns into determinate (*savikalpa*) afterwards.[80]

Jayantabhaṭṭa also suggests the inclusion of Upamāna under remembrance as an alternative. Here, the Mīmāṁsakas may argue that the memory is the recollection of the past experience and the object cognised, viz., the cow qualified by the similarity to the *gavaya* which forms the object of Upamāna was not known earlier and, hence, cannot be an object of memory. To this also, Jayantabhaṭṭa replies that the similarity is also previously cognised and consequenly the case does not exceed memory.[81] Jayantabhṭṭa further establishes that the similarity residing in the cow can be known even without knowing the similarity residing in the *gavaya*. When a person sees a *gavaya* in the forest, he does not recollect an elephant or a horse, but a cow. The memory of the cow cannot be revived without sufficient reason.[82] On the basis of this law, Jayantabhaṭṭa tries to establish that the similarlity to the *gavaya* was known earlier only and it can, therefore, be revived even when the *gavaya* is not distinctly cognised earlier. Moreover, the Mīmāṁsaka's own assessment of similarity amounts to the same. They hold that the similarity, like generality, exists wholly in each of the two members and even when the correlative of similarity is not seen, a notion of similarily is possible.[83] Even the practical utility of Upamāna postulated by the Mīmāṁsakas goes in favour of taking it as a case of memory. The Mīmāṁsakas hold that the Upamāna helps to borrow the minor details for a rite from another resembling to it. The purpose, however, is served by remembrance itself. The mention of the *Saurya* sacrifice, for example, reminds of the *Āgneya* sacrifice on account of the similarity of the deity and the meterial offered.[84] Śāntarakṣita holds that the delineation of the nature of Upamāna by the Mīmāṁsakas amounts to its inculsion under remembrance only. In the case of so called Upamāna what happens is some parts of the gavaya's body bribg about the same conceptual notion as some parts of cow's body.[85] The so called similarity is nothing but these parts. Hence, at the sight of *gavaya* there follows the remembrance of the parts of the cow's body because they are repeatedly observed.[86] That is why, the sight of *gavaya* gives rise to the memory of cow and not that of a horse.[87] The acceptance of similarity as a positive entity would not turn it different from remembrance. The similarity remembered at the sight of *gavaya* is already perceived at the time of perceiving the cow, even though the other correlative of similarity was not perceived.[88] It will again not be proper to argue that it was the similarity in general which was perceived earlier at the sight of the cow, but one cognises the similarity to *gavaya* in particular at the time of perceiving the *gavaya*. The silmilarity is essentially the same in both the cases.[89] Though the similarity was not cognised previously under a particular name at the sight of the cow, yet its cognition in its own form cannot be denied at that moment also.[90] As a matter of fact, name does not constitute the essence of an object. The cognition of the object cannot be denied in case of one who has not yet known its particular name.[91]

Vedāntadeśika suggests the inclusion of Upamāna under remembrance as one of the alternatives. The Mīmāṁsakas hold Upamāna as a means of knowing the similarity which the remembered object bears to the directly perceived one. The purpose is, however, served by remembrance. The similarity is the arrangement of the parts of the object and as such it is perceived at the time of perceiving the object itself. Thus, it is established that the similarity which the cow bears to the *gavaya* was already perceived and is remembered at the sight of the *gavaya*. This type of similarity cannot be a distinct entity also. In practice such a knowledge of similarilty seems to be new, though actually it is not so. It seems to be new on account of the limiting adjuncts in the form of the object.[92]

Śrīdhara strongly advocates the inclusion of Upamāna under remembrance. The similarity which the cow bears to the *gavaya* is remembered at the sight of *gavaya*. The perception of similarity does not require the presence of both the correlatives at a time because similarity resides in each of the correlatives.[93] Śrīdhara is aware of the objection here that remembrance is the recollection of the past experience and the similarity to *gavaya* was not cognised at the time of perceiving the cow earlier to the perception of the *gavaya*. To this he replies that the similarity is recollected at the sight of the *gavaya* through the relation of *svasaṁyukta samavāya* (inherence in the object related to it) just as the magnitudes like big or small are cognised just after perceiving the object even though the relative knowledge of size did not arise at that time. The relative knowledge arises at the time of perceiving some other object through the recollection of the size of the object perceived earlier.[94]

The Mīmāṁsakas may argue in defence of their theory that the similarity to *gavaya* was not cognised while preceiving the cow before perceiving the *gavaya* and hence, the same cannot be accepted as existing in the *gavaya*. To this also Śrīdhara replies that the rejection of the above position would further imply the rejection of the factors which account for the facts that the above mentioned similarity is cognised at the sight of the *gavaya* only and is produced in the cow only.[95] If the Mīmāṁsakas hold that the above facts are restricted through the factor of commonness of hoofs, tails, etc., to both the cow and the *gavaya* it would amount to the inclusion of Upamāna under remembrance itself. Similarity is the conglomeration of the components similar to the other object and such a similarity is already cognised at the time of perceieving the cow.[96] Such a position is supported by the following example commonly experienced in our day-to-day behaviour. There arises in a man who has not yet known the denotative relation the indeterminate knowledge of generality at the sight of one object only and the same is recognised when he comes to see some other object of that class.[97]

The above arguments, however, do not stand a critical examination. Kumārilabhaṭṭa has already established that we find the element of remembrance in Upamāna, but still it cannot be reduced to remembrance. In the stock example of the Mīmāṁsakas the similarity is perceived and the cow is remembered yet the combination of the two, i.e., the remembered cow as qualified by its similarity to *gavaya* is not cognised through remembrance.[98] The critics are under the impression that nothing new is cognised through Upamāna. In the stock example of the Mīmāṁsakas everything cognised through the perception is revived at the sight of the *gavaya*. However, they adopt different ways to explain that the similarity to *gavaya* was cognised even before the perception of the *gavaya*.

According to Bhāsarvajña, one had the indeterminate knowledge (*nirvikalpa jñāna*) of similarity which is changed into determinate knowledge at the sight of the *gavaya*,[99] The plea, however, is hardly acceptable. It does not correspond to our common experience. No one is convinced that there arises the indeterminate knowledge of similarity even without seeing the other correlative of similarity.

Jayanta's line of argument is quite powerful. From the exaperience of the remembrance of the particular object, he deduces that the similarity should be taken to be cognised earlier.[100] Here also, common experience is that what is revived at the sight of the other object is the form of the object already cognised and not its similarity or dissimilarity to the object present before the eyes. Here, Jayantabhaṭṭa puts forward that the similarity is also an assemblage of the common parts and, hence, it is remembered at the sight of the other object.[101] To this also one may argue that the position would also imply that the sight of an object gives rise to the knowledge of its similarity which cannot be stated to be the similarity to the unperceived object. Here Jayantabhaṭṭa and Śāntarakṣita hold that Kumārila's own statement that the similarity can be perceived even without the perception of one of the correlatives proves that in the stock example of the Mīmāṁsakas the perception of cow gives an idea of its similarity to *gavaya* even before perceiving the *gavaya*. The argument, however, is based upon the deduction of a wrong implication from Kumārila's statement. When Kumārila says that similarity can be perceived even without perceiving one correlate, he does not mean that it can happen even when the correlate is not known at all. The knowledge of the correlate is surely required in this case. The sight of an object can revive the knowledge of the known object only. Hence, the sight of the *gavaya* can revive the knowledge of the already perceived cow and not *vice versa*. Hence, Kumārila seems to be right when he says that the element of similarity is new in cognition. The cow, of course was perceived earlier but new the object of Upamāna is the cow as qualified by similarity and as such it is not a case of remembrance.

Śrīdhara again comes forth with an argument that one gets the notion of unrelated similarity at the sight of an object earlier to the perception of the correlative of similarity. He gives the example of the size like smaller and bigger.[102] Ānandapūrṇa rightly observes that the argument of Śrīdhara involves self cotradiction. It is contradictory to say that the object is similar to cow even when the cow is not perceived. As to the example of size, Ānandapūrṇa states that the example is not applicable to the case of similarity. The cognition of the measurement requires the knowledge of the substratum only while the knowledge of similarity requires the knowledge of the correlative of their substratum also.[103] Moreover, the usage of similarity to object is not found through the cognition of a single object only. Therefore, the similarity was not cognised earlier.[104] As to the argument of Śrīdhara regarding the factor which restricts the remembrance to the cow only at the sight of the *gavaya*, Ānandapūrṇa says that the factor is the correlative-ness of similarity.[105] Thus, the Upamāna is required to correlate in the mind of the knower the similarity residing in two objects and it cannot be a case of remembrance.

Upamāna Versus Inference

Some systematists favour the inclusion of Upamāna into inference. Amongst the Vaiśeṣikas Udayana states that the

Mīmāṁsakas postulate Upamāna as a means of cognising the similarity which the remembered object bears to the directly perceived one. They further hold that the similarity is located in every object. Hence, objects Udayana, the knowledge of similarity through the perception of similarity in some other object is a case of presumption. Since presumption is included in inference, it becomes finally a case of inference.[106] The Naiyāyikas like Jayantabhaṭṭa hold that the Mīmāṁsā view of Upamāna can be included under inference. The knowledge admitted by the Mīmāṁsakas as arising from Upamāna can be deduced through syllogism. Here, the *pakṣa* is the cow remembered at that time. The *sādhya* is the ascertainment that the remembered cow is similar to the *gavaya*. The *hetu* is 'because the former partakes of many common limbs with the second one.' The remembered cow is like the *gavaya* present before because it has many common limbs with the latter. Where there is the partaking of many common limbs with some other object, there is the similarity as in the case of twins. Here, the *hetu* does not involve any fallacy also. Thus, it can very well be included under inference.[107]

Vedāntadeśika also suggest the inclusion of Upamāna under inference as an alternative. He suggests the following form of syllogism for cognising the similarity which the remembered object bears to the directly perceived one at the sight of the latter. Whatever is similar to sime other object is the correlative of the similarity just as one hand to the other.[108] He further argues if such a position is not admitted, the knowledge of dissimilarity existing in the remembered object and known through the dissimilarity existing in the directly perceived object would require some additional means of knowledge.[109] If the dissimilarity is taken to be cognised through implication, the similarity should be taken to be cognised in the same way.[110]

Madhva states that the Upamāna postulated by other systematists as an independent means of knowledge is a particular form of inference.[111]

Jayatīrtha thinks that the inclusion of Upamāna under inference is desired with reference to a particular form of Upamāna only. He states that the Mīmāṁsakas accept three kinds of Upamāna :

(i) The means of knowing similarity which the directly perceived object bears to the remembered object.

(ii) The means of knowing the similarity which the remembered object bears to the directly perceived one, and

(iii) When the faultless statements leads to the knowledge of similarity.[112]

These are, according to Jayatīrtha, the cases of perception inference and verbal testimony respectively.[113] He discusses the inclusion of the second variety into inference. In this case the form of syllogism will be put as follows. The cow perceived earlier is similar to this *gavaya*, because that is the correlative of the similarity which the *gavaya* bears to the cow, that which is the correlative of similarity to a certain object is similar to that object; as one of the twins to the other.[114] Against the above from of syllogism, it may be argued that it involves the defect of location of the probans and the probandum at different places. The similarity which serves as a probans resides in the directly perceived object while the similarity which serves as the probandum resides in the remembered object.[115] To this also Jayatīrtha replies that the invariable concomitance is possible in the above stated manner and, hence, the difference of the above of the probans and the probandum does not become a fault.[116] Jayatīrtha further states if the sameness of abode is insisted upon, the above objection can be alleviatsd by putting the probans as—because it is correlative of the similarity abiding in the *gavaya*.[117] The form of syllogism will run like this. The cow perceived earlier is similar to this *gavaya*, because the former is the correlative of the similarity residing in the *gavaya*, as one of the twins to the other. It does not involve the defect of different locations for the probans and the probandum. The quality of being correlative of similarity abides in the cow which is also the abode of similarity which the cow itself bears to the *gavaya*. Here, it may be observed that the first form of syllogism put forward by Jayatīrtha is taken from the *Tārkikarakṣā* of Varadarāja and the rest of the portion seems to be an improvement over the same.

The Mīmāṁsakas try to prove that Upamāna expounded by them cannot be reduced to inference. Kumārilabhaṭṭa's main argument is that the conditions essential for inference are not found in the case of Upamāna. The inference requires invariable concomitance (*vyāpti*) and the presence of the probans in the *pakṣa* (*pakṣadharmatā)*. The absence of any of these conditions turns the syllogism into a fallacious reasoning. The probans should have a universal relation with the probandum and must be existent at the place of proving it. Without these qualities the probans will trun into an apparent probans (*hetvābhāsa*). Such a probans however, is not found in the present case.[118] The similarity cannot be the probans here. There is no possiblity of ascertaining the condition of the presence of the probans in the *pakṣa* because it is not cognised earlier to the rise of Upamiti as property.[119] The similarity which the *gavaya* bears to the cow also cannot serve as a probans because firstly being perceived in the *gavaya* it is not related to the cow while the probans must be related to the *pakṣa*, secondly, it serves as a part of the probandum itself. It would be absurd to say that the probandum proves a probandum.[120] The *gavaya* as qualified by the similarity to cow also cannot serve as a probans since it is in no way related to the cow and also because similarity of *gavaya* is not observed by all as invariable concomitant with the similarity to the cow. The *gavaya* is here observed for the first time and the invariable concomitance being ascertained through repeated association cannot be grasped by seeing it once.[121]

Here, the opponent comes forward with an alternative that the property of having horns, etc., found in the *gavaya* can serve as a probans. The cow will be taken as probans because the horns, etc., are concomitant with the cow and one reaches the knowledge of the cow through seeing them in the *gavaya*.[122] To this also Kumārilabhaṭṭa objects that the object of Upamāna cannot be fulfilled with that. The horns, etc., cannot bring about the knowledge of cow as bearing similarity to the *gavaya* because the function of the horns, etc., stops with the recognition of *gavaya* and as such cannot futher prove the similarity also.[123]

Kumārilabhaṭṭa further argues even if some idea is to be produced by horns, etc., the knowledge arising of it would be devoid of similarity because the cow is not similar to the horns, etc., but to the *gavaya*. The perception of the horns, etc., does not lead to the idea of the similarity of the cow to the *gavaya*.[124] In the present case what happens is this. First of all, one will perceive the horns, etc., then he will recognise the similarity of the cow to the *gavaya* and then he will arrive at the notion that the cow is similar to the *gavaya*. Thus, the first step, viz., the perception of the horns, etc., cannot directly lead to the third step.[125] Moreover, the similarity to the parts will lead to the knowledge of similarity of parts and not to that of the whole.[126] Moreover, the horns, etc., do not invariably lead to the inferential knowledge of the cow.[127] This type of inference will lead to the erroneous conclusion. The horn, etc., can be taken as the probans only if they are supposed to be perceived and the similarity which the *gavaya* bears to the cow is supposed to be unperceived. This will, however, involve many absurdities.

Firstly, it would go against the common experience because the similarity which the *gavaya* bears is taken to be uncognised though it is directly perceived.

Secondly, without the recognition of the similarity of the *gavaya* to the cow, we would not acquire through inference the knowledge of the similarity which the cow bears to the *gavaya*. It can only lead us to the notion of the cow as we know it in the village. This becomes a case of rememberance.The cow which is already perceived is remembered at the sight of the horns, etc., Thus, the knowledge of similarity which the cow bears to the *gavaya* remains out of the domain of inference.[128]

The inference depends upon the notion of non-conditioned invariable concomitance of the two objects which is again formed by repeated perception of the two toghether. In the case of Upamāna, however, this factor is not necessary. The similarity is not such a relation cognised repeatedly. In the person who has seen the cow once only and then only once the *gavaya* in the forest, the idea of similarity is produced simultaneously with the perception of *gavaya*.[129]

The probans in the case of inference requires its non-existence in the objects dissimilar to the probandum. For example, the smoke as a probans in the inference of fire requires its absence in the objects other than fire. In the case of Upamāna, however, this condition is not necessary for the supposed probans.[130]

In the case of inference the probans leads to the inferential knowledge of the probandum situated at the same place. The smoke, for example, yields the knowledge of the fire at the very locus, i.e., the probans and the probandum have the same locus. But Upamāna generates the knowledge of the object situated at some other place. The similarity, for

example, is seen in the *gavaya* but the object known is the cow situated at some other place.[131]

The causal conditions leading to Upamāna are different form those leading to inference. The cause of inference is the remembrance of the rule or nature of relation between the probans and the probandum and there is no attempt for its ascertainment. In the case of Upamāna, however, the relation is yet to be ascertained. Here, the cause is the *gavaya* endowed with the dominance of similarity with reference to the components and thus, looks only like similar.[132]

Here, it may finally be observed on our part that even if some type of faultless form of inference is found, the fact remains that such a view will not correspond to our common experience. We do not deduce this sort of fact through inference in our day-to-day behaviour. If the classification of the means of knowledge is admitted as based on our common experience, the Upamāna would not be accepted as a case of inference.

The Mīmāṁsakas also try to prove that it is not right to reject Upamāna as an independent means of knowledge on the ground that there is no object to be exclusively cognised through it. This is no ground at all. It is not necessary for a means of knowledge that its object should not be cognised through some other means. Neither is it a criterion for an object of knowledge that it should not be cognised through the other means as well.[133] The only criterion, adds *Pañcikā*, for a means of knowledge is that it should give rise to the knowledge of an object not cognised earlier. This holds good in the case of Upamāna as well. The similarity of the cow to the *gavaya* is not cognised earlier. It is this similarity which is made known through Upamāna.[134]

The critics of the Mīmāṁsā theory of Upamāna adduce some further points of criticism. Jayantabhaṭṭa states that the view of the Mīmāṁsakas regarding the nature of resultant knowledge through Upamāna lacks the support of our common experience. It is not logical to hold that the resultant knowledge is either the cow as qualified by its similarity to *gavaya* or the similarity residing in the *gavaya*. We commonly experience that the cognition of the well known object leads to the similarity residing in the unknown object and not *vice versa*. Therefore, the resultant knowledge through Upamāna may be in the form that the *gavaya* is like the cow. It does not come to one's mind that my cow is resembling to the object directly perceived.[135]

Jayantabhaṭṭa furhter proceeds to criticise the Mīmāṁsā view of the practical utility of the Upamāna. The Mīmāṁsakas hold that the Upamāna is the means of knowing the subsidiary rites and the material offered on the basis of the resemblance with some other sacrifice. The view is, however, not tenable. It is involved with internal contradiction. From the definition of the Upamāna according to the Mīmāṁsakas, it appears to be the source of cognition that the familier object is similar to the unfamiliar one, but while explaining its application, the Mīmāṁsakas city the examples which run counter to their position. From the examples offered, Upamāna becomes the source of the judgement that the unfamiliar object is like the familiar one. The *Saurya* sacrifice is said to be similar to the *Āgneya* sacrifice. The *Saurya* sacrifice is certainly unfamiliar because the details of its subsidiary rites are not given while the *Āgneya* sacrifice is familiar because the detaila of its subsidiary rites are given.[136] Moreover, the purpose of borrowing the minor details for a rite from another one resembling to it is served by memory also. The mention of the *Saurya* sacrifice, for example, reminds of the *Āgneya* sacrifice on account of the similarity of the deity and the material offered.[137] It cannot help in transforming the minor details of a certain sacrifice to the other. The Upamāna cannot play the role of the scripture and hence, cannot induce a person to perform some sacrifice.[138]

Even if Upamāna is considered so serve some purpose in sacrifice, it might have been that of the use of employing the *gavaya* in place of the cow in the sacrifice. The Mīmāṁsā view, however, does not help in this case since it gives rise to the knowledge that the cow is like the *gavaya* and not *vice-versa* which is actually required for the persent purpose. On the contrary, this purpose is served by accepting the Nyāya view of the purpose of Upamāna.[139]

Here it may be observed that Jayanta's criticism of the Mīmāṁsā view of the purpose of Upamāna shows that he has not given deep thought to it. Jayanta states that it does not go in conformity with the delineation of the nature of Upamāna. However, the defect does not arise if the position is understood like this. The person desirous of performing the sacrifice happens to go to a place where rice is not available. He sets out in search of it and comes across *nīvāra*. The sight of *nīvāra* surely reminds him of barley and when he becomes convinced that barley is not available, he gets prepared to use *nīvāra* in the place of barley. *Govardhana P. Bhatta* sides with Jayanta and states that the similarity is not a criterion for using some object as substitute as I cannot treat someone as my wife's substitute on the ground of her similarity to my wife.[140] Here, the example offered by *Govardhana P. Bhaṭṭa* does not suit the context. Moreover, if one is asked to select someone as his wife's substitute and if he gives much importance to his wife's qualities, he will prefer someone similar to his wife only. Similarly, if someone gives much importance to barley, he will select *nīvāra* as its substitute on the basis of their similarity when the former is not available.

The argument that the Mīmāṁsā view would again require some other means of knowledge for cognising dissimilarities is valid. Nārāyaṇa tries to alleviate the argument on the ground that the dissimilarity being a negation of similarity does not require some other means. However, it may be stated here that the dissimilarity is not contradictory to similarity but is contrary to it. Hence, it will not be sound to consider it as a negation of similarity. Moreover, the argument of Nārāyaṇa cannot supply a proper reply to the objection raised by Śāntarakṣita. If it is admitted that similarity as a resultant knowledge requires some distinct means, there would arise the undesirable contingency, as suggested by Śāntarakṣita, of admitting infinite number of the means of knowledge because the knowledge as 'this is first' or 'this is last' cannot be explained through any of the means of knowledge accepted by the Mīmāṁsakas.

Footnotes

1. उपमानमपि सादृश्यमसन्निकृष्टेऽर्थे बुद्धिमुत्पादयति ।
S.B.I.1.5
2. यथा गवयदर्शनं गोस्मरणस्य ।
S.B.I.1.5
3. सदृशादुपजायेत या मतिः सदृशान्तरे । ध्यानादिस्मृतितुल्यत्वात् सा नराणां कथं भवेत् ।
S.V.up.4.
4. गोस्मरणस्येति भाष्यप्रयुक्तम्, न हि स्मरणस्य बुद्धिरुत्पद्येत ।
Pañcikā, Bṛhatī, p.107
5. Epistemology of the Bhāṭṭa School of Pūrvamīmāṁsā, pp. 290-1.
6. तस्माद् यत् स्मर्यते तत् स्यात् सादृश्येन विशेषितम् ।
प्रमेयमुपमानस्य सादृश्यं वा तदन्वितम् ॥
S.V., Up.,37
7. ibid.
8. पूर्वदृष्टे स्मर्यमाणार्थे दृश्यमानार्थसादृश्यज्ञानमुपमानम्—याऽसावस्माभिर्नगरे दृष्टा गौः साऽनेन गवयेन सदृशीति ।
S.D.p.208
9. गवयस्थितसादृश्यदर्शनं करणं भवेत् ।
फलं गोगतसादृश्यज्ञानमित्यवगम्यताम् ॥
M.M.,p.110
10. गोस्मरणस्येति, अनुभूतगोः पुरुषस्य ।
Bṛhatī, p. 107

11. गोस्मरणस्येति भाष्यमयुक्तम्, न हि स्मरणस्य बुद्धिरुत्पद्यते...।

Pañcikā, p.107

12. सादृश्योत्थं ज्ञानं सादृश्यविषयमुपमानम्।

P. P., p. 267

13. दृष्टगोः पुरुषस्य तत्सदृशं गवयं पश्यतो यद्गोविषयकं गवयगतसादृश्यज्ञानं तदुपमानम्।

P. P., p. 267

14. अत्र च सादृश्यदर्शनोत्थमित्यनेनैन्द्रिकस्य सादृश्यज्ञानस्योपमानता निराकृता।

P. P., p. 270

15. P.P., p. 270-71

16. एतेनैवाऽसादृश्याद् यत्तत्सदृशभ्रान्तिविषयात् तत्सदृशविषयज्ञानं, तदप्युपमानं नाशङ्कनीयमेव, अप्रमाणत्वादित्युक्तम्।

P. P., p. 271

17. सौर्यादिवाक्यैरिहापि दृष्टम्। सादृश्यतोऽग्न्यादियुतं कथं नु प्रत्याययेदित्युपयुज्यते नः।

S. V., up. 52

18. प्रतिनिधिरपि चैवं व्रीहिसादृश्ययोगाद्
भवति तदपचारे यत्र नीवारज्ञातौ।

S.V., up. 53.

19. सादृश्यस्यापि वस्तुत्वं न शक्यमपबाधितुम्।
भूयोऽवयवसामान्ययोगो जात्यन्तरस्य तत्॥

S. V. up. 18

20. N. R. up., 18

21. सामान्यभूयस्त्वेन सादृश्यभूयस्त्वदर्शनात्।

N. R. up. 18

22. सदृशावयवत्वं तु यत्र पद्मदलाक्षिवत्।
तत् स्वावयवसामान्यभूम्ना तेषां भविष्यति॥

S. V., up. 19

23. एवं जातिगुणद्रव्यक्रियाशक्तिस्वधर्मतः।
एकै कद्वित्रिसामस्त्यभेदादेतस्य चित्रता।

S. V., up. 20

24. N. R. up. 21

25. न धर्मा एव सादृश्यं भूयस्ता वा तदाश्रयाः।

S.V. up. 21

26. यमयोः कथमेतच्चेद् दृष्टत्वात् किमिहोच्यते।
क्वचिद्धि भूयसामेतत् क्वचिदल्पीयसामपि॥

S. V. up.22

27. स मान्यानां न वा नाशः क्वचिदभ्युपगम्यते ।
सर्वस्य ह्याश्रयः कश्चिदस्ति देशान्तरादिषु ॥

S. V.up. 25

28. S. V. up. 29
29. Bṛhatī, p. 107
30. अत्र वदन्ति—सादृश्यं नाम न किंचिदस्ति द्रव्यगुणकर्मसामान्यसमवायविशेषातिरिक्तं तदन्तर्भूतं वा, तेषां सङ्ग्रहेऽपठितत्वाद्—इति पदार्थविदः।

Pañcikā, p. 107

31. सादृश्यम् इति यत्र ज्ञानम्, तत् सादृश्यम्। अस्ति चेदं ज्ञानम् तन्निबन्धना च विषयव्यवस्था।

Pañcikā, p. 107

32. Pañcikā, p. 208
33. अपि च सादृश्यस्य तत्त्वान्तरत्वे गवयेन गौर्बहुसदृशः वराहेण पुनरल्पसदृश इत्यादिप्रत्ययानां कथमुपपत्तिः।

M.M., p. 287

34. न च परिमाणभेदादल्पबहुत्वे इति वाच्यम्। द्रव्यव्यतिरिक्तस्यापरिमाणत्वात्। न चाश्रयपरिमाणभेदात् परिमाणभेदः। एकस्यैव गोराश्रयत्वात्।

M.M., p. 286

35. अस्मन्मते तु गुणावयवसामान्यानामल्पसङ्ख्याभाजां सादृश्याल्पत्वं बहुसंख्याभाजां सादृश्यबहुत्वमिति विवेकः सुकरः।

M.M., p. 287.

36. ननु सदृशतामतेर्गुणावयवसामान्यमात्रपरत्वे तदिति मतिरुत्पद्यते। अत्र तु तदिति मतिरुपजायते। यथाह भवनाथः तद्वदिति हि तद्धीः न तदिति।

M.M., p. 286

37. तदप्ययुक्तम्। गवयगतानां गुणावयवसामान्यानां गवाश्रयत्वाकारेण निरूप्यमाणानां तद्वदित्यादिबुद्धिविषयत्वं स्वरूपेण निरूप्यमाणानां तदित्यनुवृत्तकारबुद्धिविषयत्वं यथा देवदत्तो यज्ञदत्तजन्यत्वेन निरूप्यमाणो यज्ञदत्तपुत्रबुद्धिविषयो भवति स्वरूपेण तु निरूप्यमाणो देवदत्तबुद्धिमात्रो विषय इति।

M. M., p. 286-7

38. अनाश्रितस्यान्याश्रयत्वे द्रव्यत्वप्रसङ्गात्, अनन्याश्रितस्याप्ययुतसिद्धोभयव्यङ्ग्यत्वे समवायत्वप्रसङ्गात्...युतसिद्धाभिव्यङ्ग्यत्वेऽभावत्वप्रसङ्गात् गोगवयादियुतसिद्धनिष्ठाभिव्यक्त्यनुपपत्तेश्च।

N. V. T. T. P. p., 360

39. N. V. T. T. P., p. 360.
40. सत्तावतो गुणत्वापत्तेः। अग्नित्येषु च सदृशव्यवहारहानप्रसङ्गात्, अग्नित्यस्य त्वनेकाश्रयत्वे गुणवतो द्रव्यप्रसङ्गात्, निर्गुणत्वे गुणत्वप्रसङ्गात्।
N.V.T.T.P., p. 360
41. कारणत्रयविचारानुपपत्तेश्चेत्यर्थः।
N.V.T.T.P., p. 360
42. Bauddha Tarka Bhāṣā, p. 6.
43. भवतु वैषा बुद्धिस्तेन सदृशी गौरिति तथाऽपि स्मृतित्वान्न प्रमाणफलम्।
N. M. Part I, p. 133
44. N.M› Part, I p. 136
45. N.M. Part I, p. 135
46. तथा सति एतद्विसदृशोऽसावित्यस्याप्युपमानत्वापत्तेः।
Kir. p. 215
47. N. K. p. 531
48. S. T. K. 4.
49. T. S. 1542-3.
50. विज्ञातार्थप्रकाशकत्वान्न प्रमाणमियं ततः।
T.S., 1549.
51. गवयस्योपलम्भे च तुरङ्गादौ प्रवर्तते। तद्वैसादृश्यविज्ञानं यत्तदन्या प्रमा न किम्।
T. S. 1558
52. अभावान्तर्गतं नो चेन्नैवं भावावलम्बनात्।
अन्योऽन्याभावतायां वा समं सादृश्यबुद्धिषु ॥
T. S. 1559
53. सादृश्यस्य विवेको हि यथा तत्र प्रमीयते।
सर्वावयवसामान्ययोगे तत्त्वं प्रसज्यते ॥
T.S. 1561
54. भूयोऽवयवसामान्ययोगो येनाधिगम्यते।
सर्वावयवसामान्ययोगे तत्त्वं प्रसज्यते ॥
T.`S. 1561
55. एतावता च लेशेन प्रमाणत्वव्यवस्थितौ।
नेयतेता स्यात् प्रमाणानामन्यथापि प्रमाणतः ॥
T. S. 155
56. T. S. 1556-7.
57. गृहीतग्रहणान्नो चेत् समानमुपमास्वपि।
T. S. 1557
58. P. K. M., p. 346

59. ibid.
60. अन्यथागृह्यमाणगतवैसादृश्यज्ञानात् स्मर्यमाणगतवैसादृश्यप्रतीतिरपि मानान्तरं स्यात् ।

N. P., p. 490-1

61. N. P., 490
62. N. Sāra, p.73
63. N. M. Part I, p. 133
64. N. M. Part I, p. 135
65. Kir., p.215
66. N.K., p. 531
67. S. T., 5
68. T. S. 1150-51
69. P. K. M., p. 345
70. N. P., p. 490
71. Jay. on P. P.; p. 45
72. P. R. K., p.149
73. P. P. G. V., p. 218
74. S. T. K. 5
75. ibid.
76. Jay, On P.P., p. 45
77. P. R. K., p.149
78. प्रत्यक्षो गवयस्तावत् सादृश्यस्मृतिरत्र तु ।
ननु सादृश्ययुक्तेऽर्थे न स्मृतिर्नेन्द्रियाद् गतिः ।

S. V., up 7

79. N. Sāra, p. 72
80. N. Sāra, p. 73
81. गवयसादृश्यस्यापि तत्र पूर्व ग्रहणात् ।

N. M. part I, p. 133.

82. तथा हि वने गवयमालोक्य नागरिको न करेण मनुस्मरति न करभं न तुरङ्गम् अपि तु विशिष्टमेव पिण्डं न च निर्निबन्धनमेवेदं विशिष्टविषयस्मरणमुत्पत्तुमर्हति

N.M.Part I, p. 133

83. N. M. Part I, p. 133
84. ननु सौर्ये विध्यन्तार्थिनि प्रतीयमाने द्रव्यदेवतासारूप्यादेराग्नेयः स्मरणपथमवतरतीति तत एवासौ विध्यन्तमधिगच्छतीति एवमपि स्मरणमात्रात्सिद्धेऽर्थे किमुपमानेन....।

M.N. Part I, p. 136.

85. एवं तु युज्यते तत्र गोरूपावयवैः सह ।
गोरूपावयवाः केचित् तुल्यप्रत्ययहेतवः ॥

T.S. 1546

86. तत्राऽस्य गवये दृष्टे स्मृतिः समुपजायते ।
असकृद् दृष्टपूर्वेषु गोरूपावयवेष्वियम् ॥

T.S. 1547

87. T.S. 1548
88. T.S. 1550
89. तथापि स्मृतिरूपत्वं न कथञ्चिन्निवर्त्तते ।
सत्तामात्रेण विज्ञानं सादृश्यं च गवात्मनि ॥

T. S. 1551 also T. S. 1552

90. यदि नाम गृहीतं नो नाम्ना तेनैव तत् पुरा ।
गृहीतं तु स्वरूपेण यदस्यात्माऽभिधीयते ॥

T.S. 1553

91. न नाम रूपं वस्तूनां यत् तस्याग्रहणे सति ।
परिज्ञातात्मतत्त्वानामप्यविज्ञानता भवेत् ॥

T.S. 1554

92. N.P., p. 90
93. N.K., p. 531
94. N.K. p. 532
95. यदि गवि पुरा सादृश्यमिन्द्रियापातमात्रेण न गृहीतम् ? सम्प्रत्यपि गवये न गृह्यते, गवयदर्शनादेव गव्येन च स्मरणमित्युभयनियमो न स्यांदविशेषात् ।

N.K., p. 532

96. N.K., p. 533
97. दृष्टा च निर्विकल्पकगृहीतस्यापि समृतिविषयता, अव्युत्पन्नेनैकपिण्डग्रहणे प्रथमविकल्पितस्य सामान्यस्य पिण्डान्तर ग्रह्णेप्रत्यभिज्ञानात् ।

N. K., p. 533

98. प्रत्यक्षो गवयस्तावत् सादृश्यस्मृतिरत्र तु ।
ननु सादृश्ययुक्तेऽर्थे न स्मृतिर्नेन्द्रियाद्गतिः ॥

S.V. up. 7

99. N. Sāra, p. 73
100. N.M., Part I, p. 133
101. Ibid.
102. N.K., p. 532
103. N.C. p., 289
104. Ibid.

105. स्मृतिनियमश्च वस्तुतः सादृश्यप्रतियोगित्वादुपपन्नः।
N.C., p. 289

106. Kiraṇāvali, p. 215

107. N.M. part I, p. 135

108. यद्वा यो यत्सदृशः स तद्गतसादृश्यप्रतियोगी यथा मिथः स्वहस्ताविति।
N.P., p. 490

109. अन्यथा गृह्यमाणगतवैसादृश्यज्ञानात् स्मर्यमाणगतवैसादृश्यप्रतीतिरपि मानान्तरं स्यात्।
N.P., p. 490-91

110. सा चेदर्थापत्तिः सादृश्यधीरपि तथा किन्न स्यादिति।
N.P., 41

111. अर्थापत्त्युपमे अनुमानविशेषः।
P.P., p. 44

112. Jay on P.P., p. 45

113. तदेतत् त्रयं क्रमेण प्रत्यक्षाद्यन्तर्भूतम्।
Jay. on P.P., p. 45

114. Jay. on P.P., p. 45

115. नन्वनुभूयमानगतत्वेन प्रतीयमानं सादृश्यं करणम्। स्मर्यमाणगतं प्रमेयम्।तत्कथमनयोर्व्यधिकरणयोर्लिङ्गलिङ्गिभाव इति चेत्...
P.Pad., p. 17-8

116. यो यत्सदृशः स तत्सदृशः यथा यमो यमेतरेणेति व्याप्तिसंभवेन व्यधिकरणस्यादोषत्वात्।
P. Pad., p. 18

117. एतद्गवयगतसादृश्यप्रतियोगित्वस्य वा लिङ्गत्वेन सामानाधिकरण्यञ्चेति।
P. Pad., p. 18

118. न चैतस्यानुमानत्वं पक्षधर्माद्यसम्भवात्।
S.V.up. 43

119. प्राक् प्रमेयस्य सादृश्यं न धर्मत्वेन गृह्यते।
S.V. up. 43

120. गवये गृह्यमाणं च न गवामनुमापकम्।
प्रतिज्ञार्थैकदेशत्वाद् गोगतस्य न लिङ्गता॥
S. V. up. 44

121. गवयश्चान्यसम्बन्धान्न गोर्लिङ्गत्वमृच्छति।
सादृश्यं न च सर्वेण पूर्वं दृष्टं तदन्वयि॥
S. V. up. 45

122. श्रृङ्गित्वादेरथोच्येत सम्बन्धाल्लिङ्गता गवि ।

S.V. up. 47

123. तेषां गवयज्ञानव्‌यापारं प्रत्युपक्षयात्‌ ।

S. V. up. 47

124. यदि तेभ्यः प्रतीतिः स्यान्निसादृश्यैव सा भवेत्‌ ।
न गौः श्रृङ्गादिसदृशी सदृशी गवयेन तु ।

S. V. up. 48

125. सदृशप्रत्ययं दृष्ट्‌वा श्रृङ्गादिप्रत्ययात्‌ परम्‌ ।
गवयप्रत्ययादेव गोज्ञानमुपजायते ॥

S. V. up 49

126. सदृशावयवे तु तेषामेवोपमा भवेत्‌ ।

S.V. up. 50

127. न च श्रृङ्गादयो यत्र तत्र गौरनुमीयते ।

S.V. up. 50

128. इत्थं चानुमिमानस्य भ्रान्तज्ञानं प्रसज्यते ।
नगरस्थे तु गोज्ञानं स्मरणान्नातिंवर्तते ॥

S.V. up.51

129. किञ्च असकृदृष्टसम्बन्धो ह्यनुमानस्य हेतुः ।

Bṛhatī, p.108

130. असजातीयव्यावृत्तिसव्यपेक्षश्च ।

Bṛhatī, p. 108

131. अयमेव विशेषो धूमादिभिः यद्भिन्नधर्मिधर्मभूतौ गम्यगमकौ, अनुमाने हि धूमादिर्हि यत्र दृष्टः तत्र ज्ञानमुत्पादयति, एतच्च एकदेशान्तरे ।

Pañcikā, p. 107

132. ज्ञातसम्बन्धनियमश्च हेतुः । न गोगतेन सादृश्येन सह कश्चिदपि गवयवर्तिर्नस्सादृश्यस्य सम्बन्धोऽस्तीति कुतस्तरां तस्य सम्बन्धनियमावगमः ?

Prakaraṇa Pañcikā. p. 269

133. ननु चात्र प्रमेयमेव नास्तीति केचिन्मन्यन्ते तदयुक्तम्‌ । अनुभूतमपि कारणान्तरावगम्यं प्रमेयमेवेत्युक्तम्‌ ।

Bṛhatī, p. 109

134. Pañcikā 109

135. प्रसिद्धेन हि सादृश्यमप्रसिद्धस्य गम्यते ।
गवा गवयपिण्डस्य न तु युक्तो विपर्ययः ॥

N.M. Part I, p. 133

136. प्रसिद्धेनाप्रसिद्धस्य सादृश्यमवगम्यत इत्येष भवद्भिरुत्सृष्टः पन्थाः विपर्ययस्तु आश्रितः ।

N.M.PartI, p. 136

137. N.M.Part I, p. 136

138. किं चोपमानप्रतिपादितार्थो नचोदनालक्षणतां बिभर्ति ।

N.M.Part I, p. 36

139. भवत्यङ्गं यागे क्वचन गवयालम्भनमतः
तदाकारज्ञाने प्रदिनिधिविवेके च कृतिनाम् ।
उपायत्वं युष्मत्कथितमुपमानं न भजते
परिग्राह्यं तस्मात्प्रवरमुनिगीतं सुमतिभिः ।

N.M.Part I, p. 136

140. Epistomology of the Bhāṭṭa School of Pārvamīmāṁsā, p. 308

CHAPTER 4

Advaita Vedānta Concept of Upamāna

The Advaita school of Uttaramīmāṁsā accepts six means of knowledge and gives an independent status to Upamāna. We do not come across a detailed discussion of the theory of knowledge in the early texts of the Advaita Vedānta. A systematic record of the means of knowledge is given by Ānandapūrṇa Munīndra also called Ānandapūrṇa Vidyāsāgara in his Nyāyacandrikā and also by Dharmarāja Adhvaryu in his Vedāntaparibhāṣā. The present discussion is based upon these treatises on Advaita Vedạnta.

Ānandapūrṇa defines Upamiti as the knowledge of similarity which the object situated at a distance bears to that present near the observer.[1] While explaining the psychological process in Upamāna Ānandapūrṇa stated that the resultant knowledge through Upamāna refers to the cow qualified by the similarity to *gavaya*.[2] Dharmarāja Adhvaryu defines Upamāna as the instrument (*karaṇa*) of Upamiti which in turn is the resultant knowledge in the from of similarity.[3] Ānandapūraṇa explains the position with the help of the following example containing the psychological process involved in Upamāna. When a person perceives a cow in the village and comes across a *gavaya* in the forest, he comes to understand that the object perceived is like the cow. After this, he reaches the ascertainment that my cow is like the object perceived and thus, arises the knowledge of cow as qualified by its similarity to the *gavaya*.[4] Here, the means of Upamiti is the knowledge (perception) of the *gavaya*, the resultant knowledge is that of the cow as qualified by its similarity to the *gavaya* and the object of knowledge is the cow qualified by its similarity to *gavaya*.[5]

According to Dharmarāja Adhvaryu, however, the instrumentality is the knowledge of the similarity which the *gavaya* bears to the cow and the resultant knowledge is the knowledge of similarity which the cow bears to the *gavaya*.[6] The difference regarding the nature of resultant knowledge is prompted by the alternatives suggested by Kumārilabhaṭṭa that the resultant knowledge refers to the similarity or the object qualified by similarity.[7] Ānandapūrṇa accepts both the alternatives while Dharmarāja Adhvaryu accepts the former only. The psychological process involves four steps. First of all there is the knowledge or perception of points of similarity in the *gavaya*. Secondly, through the similarity is revived the memory of the cow seen earlier in the village. Thirdly, there arises the knowledge that the perceptible *gavaya* is like the cow and lastly there is the consequent cognition that the cow seen earlier is similar to the *gavaya* seen at present, or, in other words, the cow seen earlier is qualified by the similarity to the *gavaya* seen at present.

The followers of the Advaita Vedānta try to establish the independent position of Upamāna. The knowledge of the cow qualified by its similarity to the *gavaya* cannot be a case of perception. It may be admitted that the similarity is perceived through sense-object contact which makes it a case of perception, but still, it cannot be a case of perception. The knowledge of cow as qualified by its similarity to *gavaya* is not perceived at the time of knowing it. Therefore, it remains to be classed apart.[8]

It cannot be a case of inference as well. Those who are in favour of including it under inference put forth the following reasoning to show that the resultant knowledge supposed to be acquired through Upamāna acquired through inference also. My cow bears the similarity to this *gavaya*, because of having hoofs and tails, etc., as this *gavaya*.[9] Ānandapūrṇa states that here the process of reasoning is defective. The instance is not applicable to the probandum. The instance implies that the *gavaya* is similar to this *gavaya*. This is however, wrong. The same thing cannot be similar or dissimilar to itself. Thus, the fact established through such an instance goes against our common experience.[10] Dharmarāja Adhvaryu further adds that the knowledge of similarity cannot be acquired through inference because the similarity which the *gavaya* bears to the cow cannot serve as a mark or probans in inference.[11] Here, one may argue that the judgement that my cow is like the *gavaya* can be derived syllogistically. The similarity which the *gavaya* bears to the cow can very well serve as a probans in inference when the required syllogism is put like this. My cow is similar to this because she is the correlative of the similarity which the *gavaya* bears to her and whatever is correlative of the similarity to another is similar to that just as Caitra which is the correlative of similarity which Maitra bears to him is similar to Maitra.[12]

To this Dharmarāja Adhvaryu replies that even the form of syllogism is not actually observed in our common life as leading to the knowledge that my cow is similar to the *gavaya* persent before. On the contrary, the similarly which the cow bears to the *gavaya* is cognised through common experience and is not deduced through syllogism. Moreover, the *anuvyavasāya* which determines the nature of the means of knowledge is in the form that 'I know through similarity' and not through the function of the syllogism.[13]

Ānandapūrṇa further tries to disprove the inclusion of Upamāna under remembrance (*smṛti*). The main upholders of the view that the Mīmāṃsā view of Upamāna is not different from *smṛti* are Śrīdhara and Bhāsarvajña. Ānandapūrṇa records the view of Śrīdhara as follows. The knowledge that my cow is similar to this *gavaya* is a case of remembrance (*smṛti*). Such a knowledge can arise even at the sight of *gavaya* in the absence of cow. The similarity, unlike the conjunction, resides in each of its correlatives at the time of apprehending the similarity.[14] Nor should it be argued here that the remembrance is the result of the past impression and such a case does not hold good before the perception of the *gavaya*. The notion of unrelated similarity does arise at the time of perceiving the cow. It is revived at the sight of *gavaya* through the relation of *svasaṁyuktasamavāya* (inherent in the object related to the senses). The case is analogous to the knowledge like 'this is bigger than that'. Here the notion of unrelated big or small measurement arises at the time of perceiving a single object only and is revived at the sight of the other object.[15] If it is argued that similarity was not cognised through sense object contact and, hence, should not be accepted as a case of remembrance, it would pose the further problem regarding the factor which gives rise to the remembrance of cow only at the sight of *gavaya* and not of some other object.[16]

Ānandapūrṇa, however, criticises the above position on the following grounds. The knowledge of similarity can never arise without the knowledge of the correlatives of similarity. Moreover, the position of Śrīdhara involves self-contradiction. It is contradictory to say that the object is similar to cow even when the cow is not directly perceived.[17] The instance of the cognition of bigger or smaller size, offered by Śrīdhara, does not prove the case. The example is correct in itself but cannot prove the case of similarity as well. The cognition of measurement cannot be exactly similar to the cogntion of similarity. There are some objects which require the knowledge of their substratum only while there are some other objects which require the knowledge of correlatives of the substratum for thier comprehension. The first category comprises the object like measurement and the second comprises the object like similarity. The above fact is deduced from our common experience. It is observed that the measurement requires the knowledge of its substratum only for its cognition and the usage of bigger or smaller depends upon that only, while the knowledge of similarity depends upon the cognition of the correlatives of its substratum. The usage of similarity to some object is not found through the cognition of single object. Therefore, the similarity was not cognised earlier and there can be remembrance wiithout the earlier cognition.[18] It is also wrong to say that the non-determinate knowledge of the object also can give rise to recognition.[19] As regards the factor which causes the remembrance of cow only at the sight of *gavaya*. Ānandapūrṇa says that the factor here is the correlativeness of similarity. The sight of *gavaya* causes the remembrance of the cow only because of the similarity.[20] Thus, it is established that the cogintion of similarity which the distant object bears to the near one requires a distinct means.[21]

Ānandapūrṇa further adduces the following arguments to prove that Upamāna cannot be a case of remembrance (*smṛti*). The remembrance is the result of the past impression of the objects. The knowledge of the cow qualified by the similarity cannot be the result of the past impression because the *gavaya* and consequently its similarity to cow was not perceived earlier to the perception of the *gavaya*.[22] The opponent comes forward with the following objection. The similarity is like the class character of cow (*gotva*). The identity of similarity with the class-character cannot be denied because the similarity like the class-character is eternal and inherent in many objects of the class. The similarity also, like the class-character and through existing in many individual objects, is perceived at the sight of a single object only, because all the causal conditions leading to its perception are present. Otherwise, the similarity cannot be cognised in the *gavaya* also. As such, the similarity was perceived at the sight of the cow itself and is remembered at the time of perceiving the *gavaya*.[23] Ānandapūrṇa cuts the very root of the argument and establishes that the similarity cannot be identified with the class-character. If it is identical with the class-character, it would be defined as the commonness of various constituent parts and properties of merely the generality. Both of these alternatives cannot explain the exact nature of similarity. The first does not hold good because the similarity is found even in the object having no components or property. For example, we find the similarity between the smell of *ketaki* and that of the snake, though the smell is devoid of the components and properties. The knowledge of similarity cannot be invalid also since it is not sublated. The second alternative also cannot be accepted because it would involve undesirable contingency of admitting everything similar to everything because all the objects in general have the common character of being objects of knowledge as also the existence.[24] The following fact also leads to the difference between similarity and class-character. Similarity, like negation, etc., is made known by its correlatives while the class-character does not depend upon many objects of class because the causal conditions for the knowledge of the class-character can be perceived at the time of perceiving an object. The knowledge of similarity, however, depends upon the knowledge of correlatives and cannot be comprehended by the same causal conditions as the object itself. Hence it can be said that the class-character of cow which is made known by the individual cow was perceived earlier but not its similarity to the *gavaya* because the *gavaya* was not perceived. The causal conditions leading to the knowledge of similarity were not present earlier and hence, it was not perceived earlier.[25]

Moreover, the definition of class-character is not applicable to similarity. Firstly, the defintion of class-character should be as inherent in many objects but such a relation of inherence is not admitted by the Vedāntins. Secondly, the defintion of class-character further requires that the property should be common to many objects. It would give rise to the undesirable contingency of admitting many qualities as class-character because they are common to many objects.[26]

The objector again puts forth the following plea to include Upamāna under remembrance. Firstly, the sight of cow gives the indeterminate. (*nirvikalpa*) knowledge of similarity even without its correlative. The knowledge of the correlative is necessary for the determinate (*savikalpa*) knowledge of similarity. The indeterminate knowledge of similarity is acquired even earlier to the perception of *gavaya* and as such it becomes the case of remembrance. The knowledge of cow characterised by its similarity to *gavaya* also is acquired earlier and, thus, it becomes a case of remembrance.[27] Secondly, the similarity is the possession of hoof, tail, etc., common to both the cow and the *gavaya*. These are, however, perceived earlier. Therefore, the knowledge of cow as characterised by its similarity to *gavaya* becomes a case of remembrance only.[28] Ānandapūraṇa strikes at the root of the argument stating that it is wrong to hold that the indeterminate knowledge of similarity arises without the knowledge of the correlatives of similarity. There is no proof to establish that the knowledge of correlative is necessary only in the case of determinate knowledge of similarity.[29] As regards the second argument Ānandapūrṇa states that the argument is based upon wrong notion of similarity. It is wrong to say that the similarity is nothing but the component parts of the body of the cow because the similarity is observed in case of the objects having no component parts and properties as in the case of smell.[30] Therefore, it is settled that Upamāna cannot be reduced to remembrance. Ānandapūraṇa directs these arguments against the view of Bhāsarvajña a Naiyāyika who refutes Upamāna as an independent means of knowledge.[31]

Upamāna cannot be reduced to presumption (*arthāpatti*) also. Ānandapūrṇa presents the opponents stating that Upamāna can be reduced to presumption through the following reasoning. If my cow would not be similar to it, there would not arise the knowledge that the *gavaya* is similar to that, because the similarity is located in both the correlatives. This *gavaya* is found to be similar to the cow. Hence, it means by implication that my cow also is similar to it.[32] This reasoning, states Ānandapūrṇa, is not correct. It would go against the position of the opponent himself because it would be a case of remembrance. The knowledge of similarity which the distant object bears to the present one would naturally refer to perceived earlier and such a knowledge would be a case of remembrance. To make it a case of persumption would imply the contradicion to the above fact.[33] Moreover, it poses the further problem whether it is valid that the similarity which the present object bears to the distant one is pervaded by that located in the distant object or not.

The first alternative does not stand because there is no means to prove it. It cannot be established through perception because the similarity which the distant object bears is not in contact with the senses and as such the cognition of pervasiveness which requires the repeated perception of two together cannot be ascertained. Nor can it be ascertained through some probans for the invariable concomitance is not observed in the present case. Nor is it ascertained through the verbal testimony becausse the verbal testimony is not a factor to decide the invariable concomitance. The invariable concomitance is observed in absence of the authoritative statement also. Since the presumption is based upon invariable concomitance, it cannot comprise Upamāna also. The second argument leaves no scope for similarity and, hence, cannot make Upamāna a case of presumption. Therefore, it is established that Upamāna cannot be included under presumption.[34] Here, the supporters of the inclusion of Upamāna under presumption come forward with the following plea. The similarity residing in the object can be knowledge that this object is smaller or bigger than the other. When one observes an object, he gets an idea that 'it is bigger than that and that is smaller than this' through presumption. The bigger size of that cannot be justified without the smaller size of this. Similarly, the similarity of this to that cannot be justified without the similarity of that to it. In this way, the knowledge of similarity becomes a case of presumption.[35] To this, Ānandapūrṇa replies that the instance of ter cognition of smaller or bigger size cannot properly be applied to the case of similarity. In the case of the cognition of the smaller or bigger size, the process is like this. The size of the object is perceived earlier without perceiving the correlative and perceiving the other object one gets the knowledge of the smaller or bigger size. This is due to the perception of the object in association with the impression of the object perceived in the past. At the sight of the present object, one remembers the distant object and thus acquires the knowledge of the smaller or bigger size of the object. The case is analogous to the letters of a word which give rise to the knowledge at the time of uttering the letter with the impression of the letters uttered earlier. The similarity however, cannot be cognised without the correlarives. Hence, it cannot be deduced through presumption.[36]

Ānandapūrṇa further alleviates the objection that the acceptance of Upamāna as an independent means would imply the acceptance of some other independent means for knowing dissimilarity also. He states that the dissimilarity may be understood either in the sense of absence properties belonging to some other object or the presence of some properties peculiar to the object itself. The first can be exemplified as the absence of the factor differentiating buffalo from the cow. When the cow is said to be different from buffalo; this kind of similarity is obviously a case of negation and, thus, is cognised through non-perception.[37] The second interpretation can be exemplified as the buffaloness (the character of being a buffalo). If this kind of peculiar characteristic is already cognised and is remembered as non-existent in the cow at the sight of the *gavaya*, it becomes a case of remembrance (*smṛti*)[38]. Or again, when this kind of dissimilarity (i.e., absence of peculair characteristics of buffalo is understood to be existing in the cow, the experience arises in the form that peculiar charcteristics of buffalo do not exist in the cow and, thus, such a knowledge of dissimilarity arises obviously through non-perception only.[39] Therefore, there arises no undesirable contingency of admitting some additional means for cognising dissimilarity.

Ānandapūrṇa supports the stand of the Prābhākara school of Pūrvamīmāṁsā that similarity is a distinct object. It should not be argued that similarity does not exist at all. the existence of similarity is established through the experience that this object is similar to that.[40] The non-existence of similarity cannot be deduced from its non-inclusion under the categories like substance, etc. What meant here is that all the objects can be classified into these categories only and the non-inclusion of any object into these implies its non-existence. Here, the from of inference, says Ānandapūrṇa, involves the defect of the non-existence of the substratum itself. Consequently there remains no substratum for the existence of the probans in this case.[41] If, for the sake of argument, some substratum is admitted, it would imply the existence of the similarity also because the substratum will obviously be qualified by similarity and as such it would imply the existence of the qualification also.[42] Ānandapūrṇa concludes the argument by citing the authority of Śālikanātha that the similarity as an object knowledge is established through the cognition of similarity. Hence, similarity exists as a positive category different from substance, etc.[43]

In this context it should be noted that the Advaita school of Uttaramīmāṁsā accepts the essentials of Upamāna as postulated by the Pūravamīmāṁsā, but still, the practical utility of Upamāna accepted by the Pūrvamīmāṁsa may not be accepted by the Advaitins. The sole purpose of Vedānta unlike the Pūramīmāṁsā, is not fulfilled with the ritualistic interpreta-tion of the scriptural statements. On the other hand, the Vedānta system aims at providing the correct interpretation of scriptural statements regarding the knowledge of ultimate reality. Therefore, it will not be consistent with the spirit of the Vedānta system to say that Upamāna serves the purpose of replacing one object with the other similar to it in the context of the sacrificial rites. Nor can it be said that Upamāna is postulated here in order to establish the dissimilarity of Brahman to the wordly objects because Upamāna is a means of knowing similarity rather than dissimilarity. Hence, the purpose of Upamāna should be accepted as the explanation of the analogy of the common experience. There are many statements in the Upaniṣads which indicate the similarity of the unobserved fact to the observed one. Upamāna may be accepted as a means of the correct interpretation of these passages. When the supernatural expreience is said to be similar to the common experience, the experssion speaking of the common experience is remembered and this leads to the similarity of two levels of experience.

Footnotes:

1. सन्निकृष्टेनासन्निकृष्टस्य सादृश्यमिति उपमितिः ।

N.C.,p. 279

2. सादृश्यविशिष्टगोज्ञानमुपमितिः ।

N.C., p. 279

3. तत्र सादृश्यप्रमाकरणमुपमानम् ।

V.P., p. 192.

4. N.C., p.279. Cf. V.P., p. 192
5. तत्र गवयज्ञानमुपिमितिकरणम् । गवयसादृश्यविशिष्टगोज्ञानमुपमितिः । गवयसादृश्यविशिष्टा गौः प्रमेयम् ।

N.C., p. 279

6. तत्रान्वयव्यतिरेकाभ्यां गवयनिष्ठगोसादृश्यज्ञानं करणम् । गोनिष्ठगवयसादृश्यज्ञानं फलम् ।

V.P., up. 192

7. S.V., up. 37
8. N.C., p.280; V.P. p. 194
9. मदीया गौः एतत्सादृश्यवती खुरपुच्छादिमत्त्वाद् एतद्गवयवद् इत्यनुमानादस्तु तत्सिद्धिरिति चेत् ।

N.C.,p. 283

10. न, साध्यविफलत्वाद् दृष्टान्तस्य । न ह्ययं गवय एतत्सदृशः । अन्यस्यान्येन सादृश्यं वैसादृश्यं वा न स्वेनैव, प्रसिद्धिविरोधात् ।

N.C., p. 283

11. नाप्यनुमानेन, गवयनिष्ठगोसादृश्यस्यातल्लिङ्गत्वात् ।

V. P., p. 194

12. नापि मदीया गौरेतद्गवयसदृशी, एतन्निष्ठसादृश्यप्रतियोगित्वाद् यो यद्गतसादृश्यप्रतियोगी स तत्सदृशः, यथा मैत्रनिष्ठसादृश्यप्रतियोगी चैत्रः मैत्रसदृश इत्यनुमानात्तत्सम्भव इति वाच्यम् ।
13. एवंविधानुमानानवतारेऽप्यनेन सदृशी मदीया गौरिति प्रतीतेरनुभवसिद्धत्वात् । उपमिनोमीत्यनुव्यवसायाच्च

V.P., p. 196

14. N.C., p. 288
15. यदि गवि पुरासादृस्यमिन्द्रियापातमात्रेण न गृहीतम्, तदा गवयदर्शनादेव गवये च स्मरणमित्युभयनियमो न स्याद् अविशेषात्.......... ।

N.C. p. 288-9

17. तदयुक्तम् सादृश्यप्रतियोगितीतिमात्रमन्तरेण प्रतीत्यभावनियमात् । गोपिण्डस्यादर्शनेऽपि गोसदृशोऽयमिति प्रतीयत इति स्ववचनविरोधाच्च ।

N.C., p.289

18. N.C., p. 289

19. निर्विकल्पकेन गृहीतत्वेनाप्रत्यभिज्ञानात् ।

N.C., p. 289

20. स्मृतिनियमश्च वस्तुतः सादृश्यप्रतियोगित्वादुपपन्नः ।

N.C., p. 289

21. तदेवं सन्निकृष्टेनासन्निकृष्टस्य सादृश्यमित्युपमानं मानानन्तरमिति ।

N.C., p. 289

22. विशिष्टस्यान्यतोऽसिद्धेरुपमानप्रमाणता ।

N.C., p. 280 and

सादृश्यस्यावगमायोगाद् गवयावगमात् पुरा तज्ज्ञानं न स्मृतिः

N.C., p. 281

23. N.C., p. 280
24. N.C., p. 281-2
25. गोत्वस्य तु युक्तं प्रथमत एव ग्रहणं प्रतियोग्यनिरूप्यस्वभावम्, व्यक्त्या समानसामग्रीत्वाच्च सादृश्यस्य च पुनः प्रथमत एवोपलम्भसामग्र्यभावः प्रतियोगिवाक्यग्रहणाभावात् ।

N.C., p. 282

26. N.C., p. 282
27. N.C., p. 283
28. N.C., p. 283
29. N.C., p. 283
30. अवयवगतखुरपुच्छादिमत्त्वस्य सादृश्यपदवाच्यत्वमपि निरवयवगन्धादिसादृश्य-प्रदर्शनेनापास्तम् ।

N.C., p. 283

31. Cf. N.C., p. 284
32. नोपमानं मानान्तरम् अर्थापत्तितस्तत्सिद्धेः । यद्यनेन सदृशी सा न स्यात्, ततस्तया सदृशोऽयं नोपलभ्येत, सदृशस्योभयनिष्ठत्वात् । उपलभ्यते चायं तया सदृशः

N.C., p. 286

33. तदसत्, असन्निहितसादृश्यधीः स्मृतिरिति प्रतिज्ञाविरोधात् ।

N.C., p. 286

34. N.C., p. 286
35. N.C., p. 286-7
36. N.C., p. 287
37. गवयनिष्ठधर्माभावो महिषे वैधर्म्यमनुपलब्ध्या गम्यम्, अभावत्वात् ।

N.C., p. 287

38. तन्मात्रनिष्ठं महिषत्वादिकमपि पूर्वगृहीतमेतद्ग्रहणानन्तरं स्मर्यते ।
N.C., p. 207

39. तस्या च वैधर्म्यरूपत्वं गवयनिष्ठत्वाभावरूपमनुपलब्ध्यैवानुभूयते ।
N.C., p. 287

40. न च सादृश्यमेव नास्तीति साम्प्रतम्, सदृसोऽयमित्यनुभवसिद्धत्वात् ।
N.C., p.279

41. N.C., p. 279

42. सिद्धौ वा धर्मिग्राहकप्रमाणबाधात् ।
N.C., 279

43. N.C., p. 279

CHAPTER V

Bhāsarvajña on Upamāna

Unlike rest of the Naiyāyikas, Bhāsarvajña does not admit Upamāna as an independent means of knowledge. He rejects the view of the syncretist Naiyāyikas as well as that of the Mīmāṁsakas and includes Upamāna envisaged by them into other means of knowledge.

As regards the view of the syncretist Naiyāyikas, Bhāsarvajña holds that neither the nature of the means nor that of the restultant knowledge proves Upamāna as an independent means of knowledge. The acceptance of Upamāna as an independent means of knowledge on the basis of conveying similarity would lead to the undesirable contingency of admitting as many means of knowledge as the objects because every individual object would require a distinct means for the determination of the denotative relation.[1] Bhāsarvajña finally includes Upamāna under verbal testimony and claims that his position brings forth the true nature of the intention of the author of the *Nyāyasūtras*. The *sūtrakāra* does not intend to establish Upamāna as an independent means of knowledge but mentions it on account of its serviceableness to prove the validity of verbal testimony.[2] It is enumerated to refute the objection that a sentence cannot give the knowledge of the objects which are neither perceptible nor inferable because the sentence communicates the knowledge of the relation of the objects denoted by it which are already known. Upamāna serves as an example against such an objection. Just as the denotative relation is established by a sentance expressing similarity, the denotative relation in case of the objects beyond perception like *Śakra*, can be established in various ways like similarity.[3] As for the discussion of the validity of Upamāna in the *sūtras* of Gautama *Bhāsarvajña* says that the discussion is made to show that Upamāna, like presumption, is valid but is included into other means of knowledge.[4]

Regarding the *sūtrakāra's* effort to establish that Upamāna is not a case of inference, Bhāsarvajña holds that this cannot be taken as his objection to the inclusion of Upamāna under verbal testimony also.[5] As to the statement of Gautama that there are four means of knowledge, Bhāsarvajña states that here what Gautama means is that they are not five or more.[6] As to the query why the *sūtrakāra* does not state that there are only three means of knowledge, Bhāsarvajña replies that here the *sūtrakāra* does not state his view carefully. This kind of carelessness is found at many places in the *sūtras*. For example, while refuting the idea of whole through the discussion of the alternatives of the whole and the part, he seems to refute the very existence of the whole while what he really means is that the whole exists separately from the parts.[7]

Moreover, there is no common experience of some knowledge as derived through Upamāna. When a person is asked how he knew the *gavaya* or its name, the answer is through the words of the forester. There is no answer that it was through Upamāna.[8] Bhāsarvajña further rejects the notion that the knowledge of denotative relation cannot arise until the object denoted is not directly perceived. It is experienced in our common behaviour that the name of the object is known even in the absence of its perceptive knowledge. Otherwise, there would arise the undersirable contingency of admitting distinct means for the cognition that it is denoted by the name cow, even after knowing this is cow.[9]

Bhāsarvajña rejects the Mīmāṁsā view of considering Upamāna as a distinct means of knowledge and holds that it is not different from remembrance (*smṛti*). The perception of the cow earlier also involves the perception of her similarity to the unknown animal as well, for the similarity is inherent in the cow itself. Thus, the cow as qualified by its similarity to *gavaya* was already perceived at the sight of the cow itself.[10] When one saw the cow, he had the abstract (*nirivikalpa*) knowledge of the similarity while the perception of the *gavaya* turns it into determinate (*savikalpa*). The perception of the *gavaya* revives the similarity already received and, thus, it becomes a case of remembrance. In the other cases also it is experienced that the indeterminate knowledge gives rise to the determinate remembrance. For example, we have the knowledge of the presence of some persons at some place, we get the indeterminate knowledge of the absence of particular person but the same knowledge turns into determinate knowledge of that particular person when asked by others.[11]

Footnotes :

1. गोपिण्डान्तरेऽपि सङ्केतग्रहणे प्रमाणान्तराभिधानप्रसङ्ग इति ।
N.Sāra, p. 73.
2. शब्दप्रमाणसमनार्थ प्रयोजनम् ।
N.Sāra, p. 75
3. N. Sāra, p.76
4. परीक्षा त्वर्थापत्तिवत्प्रमाणस्य सतः प्रमाणेष्वन्तर्भावज्ञापनार्थमिति ।
N.Sāra, p. 76.
5. अन्तर्भावस्त्वनुमान एवास्य यथाश्रुतोऽपि निराकृतो नागम इति ।
N.Sāra, p. 76.
6. चतुष्पदाभिधानं सूत्रेषु पञ्चत्वादिनिराकरणार्थं न त्रित्वप्रतिषेधार्थम् ।
N.Sāra, p. 76
7. N.Sāra, p. 77

8. प्रश्नोत्तराभिधानादन्यप्रमाणनिर्देशाच्च ।

N.Sāra, p. 73

9. एवं तर्हि गौरयमित्येवं संकेते कृतेऽस्य गोशब्दः संज्ञेति प्रतिपत्तौ प्रमाणान्तरं वाच्यम् ।

N.Sāra, p. 73

10. पूर्वमेव हि सादृश्यविशिष्ट उपलब्धो गोपिण्डः ।

N.Sāra, p. 72

11. निर्विकल्पकोपलम्भाच्च संस्कारसहकारिसामर्थ्यादभावादिषु सविकल्पिका स्मृतिदृष्टेति ।

N.Sāra, p. 73

CHAPTER 6

Vaiśeṣika Concept of Upamāna

The vaiśeṣikas refuse to accept Upamāna as an independent means of knowledge. The *Vaiśeṣikasūtra* accepts only the perception and inference as the independent means of knowledge and does not refer to Upamāna. Praśastapāda states that Upamāna is the means of conveying the knowledge of *gavaya* by an authoritative person through the similarity to the cow to a person who does not know it earlier. This is, however, nothing other than verbal testimony.[1] Śrīdhara clarifies the statement more Validity and adds that since the Upamāna depends upon the validity of the speaker, it is not different from verbal testimony. Verbal testimony, however, is a case of inference. Hence, Upamāna is also a case of inference.[2] This is, according to Śrīdhara, the criticism of the view of considering the reliable authority as Upamāna.[3]

Udayana and the other commentators following him take note of both the views of Upamāna, viz., that of the Naiyāyikas and the Mīmāṁsakas. As regards the view of the Naiyāyikas, Udayana states that the statement of the authority forming the basis of Upamāna, is the verbal tastimony. The resultant knowledge, viz., the denotative relation is also arrived as through the authoritative statement.[4] It is wrong to say that one cognises the denotative relation between the word and the object *gavaya* through the similarity conveyed by the statement of the authoritative person. Otherwise, one who does not know *gavaya* would not come to know the cow also.[5] The essence of *gavaya* which leads to the knowledge of the denotative relation is not its similarity to the cow but the *gavaya-ness* which is the factor leading to the knowledge of the denotative relation. It is known by the statemant of the authoritative person himself and, hence, Upamāna is nothing but a case of verbal testimony which is further included in inference. It is also not proper to argue that the resultant knowledge through Upamāna cannot be arrived at through perception and the other means of knowledge because there is the propriety in saying that the usage regarding the denotative relation is known through the statement of the reliable person. A person knows the denotative ralation eariler and after perceiving the object, he recognises that the object present is the object denoted by that particular word.[6]

Śrīdhara shows that the Nyāya view of Upamāna as presented by Uddyotakara cannot be an independent means of knowledge. There are two elements viz., the assertion of the reliable authority and the perception of similarity. As regards the former, it is a case of verbal testimony pure and simple and the knowledge arising out of it is also verbal.[7] The similarity is also a case of perception[8]. The knowledge arising out of Upamāna is inferential. The word denotes the object with reference to which it is used by the authorities without exception. The forest-dweller uses the term *gavaya* with reference to the object *gavaya.* Hence, there arises the inferential knowledge that the object gavaya is denoted by word *gavaya.*[9] Śaṁkaramiśra thinks that the factor leading to the knowledge of denotative relation is the fact that similarity to cow and the word *gavaya* are applied to one and the same object. Here, Śaṁkaramiśra anticipates an argument that *gavayatva* which determines the use of the term *gavaya* in a particular sense is not known at the state of hearing the statement from the reliable authority and, hence, one cannot know that the term *gavaya* denotes that particular object only. To this Śaṁkaramiśra answers that the knowledge of *gavayatva* is possible through figurative sense at the time of hearing the statement.[10]

As regards the Mīmāṁsā concept of Upamāna, Udayana states that the view does not make it obligatory to accept Upamāna as an independent means of knowledge. If the knowledge of similarity is the object of Upamāna, the knowledge of dissmilarity also would be cognised through Upamāna. This serves as a reply to the argument that Upamāna should be admitted as an independent means because it cannot be included under perception, for there is no sense-object-contact and because it cannot be a case of remembrance, for the object qualified by similarity was not perceived earlier.[11] It is also not possible to take similarity as a distinct object because the similarity is not something more than resemblance of from in the components.[12] Moreover, the similarity is held to be located in every object. Hence, the cognition of the similarity in other object would better be a case of presumption (*arthāpatti*) which is again a case of inference.[13]

The knowledge of similarity, argues Śrīdhara, is a case of remembrance. Śrīdhara makes it clear that the knowledge of similarity does not require the presence of both the correlatives of similarity at a time. The Mīmāṁsakas have themselves admitted that the similarity, like generality, resides in each of the correlatives and as such it does not require the presence of both the correlatives. The knowledge of similarity can arise even when one of the correlatives is not perceived at that time. Hence, the perception of a single correlatilve, viz., *gavaya* can revive the knowledge of the similarity which the cow bears to the *gavaya*.[14] Śrīdhara is aware of the differculty that the remembrance is the recollection of the past experience and the similarity to *gavaya* was not cognisesd at the time of perceiving the cow before perceiving the *gavaya*. The similarity is recollected and knowṇ at the sight of the *gavaya* through the relation of *svasṁyuktaskamavāya* (inherent in the object related to it), just as the mangnitude like big or small are cognised just after perceiving the object even though the cognition in the form of 'bigger than that' or 'smaller than that' did not arise at that time. The cognitions in the form of bigger than that etc., arise at the time of perceiving some other object through the recollection of that residing in the object perceived earlier.[15] What Śrīdhara seems to mean is though there was no cognition of similarity which the cow bears to *gavaya* before perceiving the *gavaya*, yet the notion of unrelated similarity cannot be denied just as the unrelated knowledge of big or small mangnitude of objects arises even at the sight of a single object before perceiving the other correlative of bigger or smaller magnitude.

Śrīdhara is further aware of the objection that the similarity to *gavaya* was not cognised while perceiving the cow before perceiving the *gavaya* and, hence, the same cannot be accepted as existing in the *gavaya*. To this, Śrīdhara replies that the rejection of such a position on the ground of the above factor would further imply the rejection of the factors which account for the facts that the above-mentioned similarity is (i) cognised at the sight of *gavaya* only and (ii) is produced in the cow only. There is no ground to deny the other alternatives in these cases.[16] Here, the Mīmāṁsakas may suggest that the factor for restricting the remembrance to cow is the fact that the hoof, tale, etc., are common to both the cow and the *gavaya*. It leads to the conclusion that it is the cow only which is remembered at the sight of *gavaya*. In response to it Śrīdhara states that the similarity is the conglomeration of the components similar to the other object and as such this kind of similarity exists in both the correlatives of similarity. It means by implication that such a similarity is clearly cognised at the time of perceiving the cow. Thus, the imperession of similarity which the cow bears to the *gavaya* is revived at the time of seeing the *gavaya*. It makes it a case of remembrance only and leaves no scope for Upamāna as a distinct means of knowledge.[17] Such a position is supported by our common experience also. Some times, we remember the object of indeterminate knowledge as well. For example, there arises in the man who has not yet known the denotative relation the indeterminate knowledge of generality at the sight of one object only and the same is recognised when he comes to see some other object of that class.[18]

Footnotes :

1. आप्तेनाप्रसिद्धगवयस्य गवयस्य गवा गवयप्रतिपादनादुपनमाप्तवचनमेव ।
   P.B., Kiraṇāvali, p. 214
2. N.K., 530-31
3. ये तावत्पूर्वमीमांसका वनेचरवचनमेवोपमानमाहुस्तेषामिदमनुमानमेव ।
   N,K..,p. 531
4. यथा गौस्तथा गवय इति आप्तवचनमेव विदेशवाक्यमेवोपमानं प्रमाणमित्यर्थः। वाक्यादेव संज्ञासंज्ञिसम्बन्धपरिच्छेदस्यापि सिद्धेः।
   N.K., p. 531
5. भवेदेवं यदि सादृश्यं शब्दप्रवृत्तिनिमित्तं स्यात् ।तथा सत्यप्रतीतगूनामव्यवहारप्रसङ्गात् ।
   Kiraṇāvali, p. 215
6. Kiraṇāvali, p. 215
7. तेषामपि यथा गौर्गवयस्त थेति वाक्यं तज्जनिता च लोके य : खलु गवय इति श्रूयते सः गोसदृशः इति बुद्धिरागम एव।
   N.K., p. 533
8. प्रत्यक्षे गवये सादृश्यज्ञानं प्रत्यक्षफलम् ।
   N.K., p. 534
9. N.K., p. 534
10. अतिदेशवाक्यश्रवणसमये गवयत्वं प्रवृत्तिनिमित्तं न ज्ञातमतः कथं संज्ञापरिच्छेद इति चेद् लक्षणया तत्प्रतीतिसम्भवांत् ।
    Varśeṣikasūtropaskāra.. p. 507

11. Kiraṇāvali, p. 215
12. तथा हि न तावदस्य विषयः सादृश्यपदव्यपदेश्यं पदार्थान्तरमेव सम्भावनीयम्, सादृश्यस्य सामान्यानतिरेकात्।

    Kiraṇāvali, p. 15
13. सादृश्यैकनियतं चैतत्। अथैतदर्थापत्तिरेवेति मनोरथः...।

    Kiraṇāvali., p. 215
14. N.K., p. 531
15. N.K., p. 532
16. यदि गवि पुरा सादृश्यमिन्द्रियापातमात्रेण न गृहीतम्, सम्प्रत्यपि गवये न गृह्यते, गवयदर्शनादेव गवयेन च स्मरणमित्युभयनियमो न स्यादविशेषात्।

    N.K., p. 532
17. N.K., p. 533
18. दृष्टं च, निर्विकल्पकगृहीतस्यापि समृतिविषयता अव्युत्पन्नेनैकपिण्डग्रहणे प्रथममविकल्पिततस्य सामान्यस्य पिण्डान्तरग्रहणे प्रत्यभिज्ञानात्।

    N.K., 533

CHAPTER 7

Sāṁkhya Concept of Upamāna

The Sāṁkhyas accept perception, inference and verbal testimony only as the independent means of knowledge. The *Sāṁkhyakārikā* states that the additional means postulated by other systematists are included under these only.[1] The commentators give various explanations of the inclusion. There is the divergence of opinion regarding the inclusion of Upamāna also.

The *Yuktidīpikā* takes notice of Nyāya view of Upamāna only and includes it under verbal testimony. Mere similarity does not lead to the knowledge of some object, It is the valid statement which leads one to the knowledge arrived at through Upamāna.[2] Here, the Naiyāyikas are presented as arguing that Upamāna does require similarity in addition to the words. If it would have been identical with verbal testimony, it would lead to the valid knowledge even without the statement of similarilty. The listener understands through the sentence containting the sense of well-known similarity and not through mere words. It is also not proper to argue that Upamāna is based upon the function of words and is, therefore, included under verbal testimony. It would involve the undesirable contingency of inculsion of *vīta* and *avīta* type of inference also under verbal testimony. These also stand in need of fuction of the words for establishing some object for others.[3] To this, the *Yukītidīpikā* objects that the statement of similarity is only a mode of expression and is not a factor for making Upamāna an independent means. An intelligent speaker uses the well known similarity because otherwise the sense cannot properly be conveyed.[4] If this kind of mode is taken as a condition for an independent means of knowledge, the other modes of conveying the meaning like waving the hand and closing the eye would be independent means of knowledge.[5] Moreover, like verbal testimony, the Upamāna also depends upon the fact whether the speaker has visualised the object or not. The knowledge of the knower of *gavaya* is justified (or valid) only when the speaker is an authority.[6] Like verbal testimony, Upamāna also depends upon particular words. If it is admitted that the *gavaya* is known through the well known similarity independent of verbal operation, the knowledge of *gavaya* would arise through the statement 'as the horse, so the *gavaya*.'[7]

The acceptance of Upamāna for the sake of comprehending the denotative relation would also to the undesirable contingency of infinite regress with reference to the number of pramāṇas because all the other types of stetment leading to the denotative relation will have to be considered as distinct means of knowledge. For example, the Naiyāyikas will have to admit some independent means for such cognition as among the persons sitting here Devadatta is he who is wearing a wreath, is decorated with ear-ring, has a board chest, and has red and longish eyes.[8] Moreover, when after seeing both the cow and the *gavaya* one thinks that 'as is the cow so is the *gavaya*' (i.e., both are similar to each other), this kind of knowledge would not be a true or valid knowledge since it is cognised through some other means. The Naiyāyikas hold that the valid knowledge is the valid experience in contradication to the remembrance which is the result of past impressions. In the present case, the knowledge is fresh and valid but still it does not come under the Nyāya definition of valid knowledge because they will accept it as cognised earlier through some other means.[9]

in accordance with the stress laid upon the particular aspect of Upamāna. It is a case of inference if the stress is laid upon the similarity conveyed through the authoritative statement. One arrives at a universal relation that the animal similar to cow is *gavaya* through the authoritative statement and seeing the similarity to the cow in the *gavaya* he comes to the conclusion through the cognition of pervasion that the object before him is denoted by the word *gavaya*.[17] It is a case of remembrance (and consequently the preception) if the stress is laid upon the perception of the similarity cognised earlier.[18] It is a case of verbal testimony if the stress is laid upon the authoritative statement since the knowledge in this case is sentence-generated.[19]

Footnote :

1. तानि प्रमाणानि प्रत्यक्षानुमानशब्दाख्यानि त्रीणि ।
   Y.M.D., p. 8
2. N.P., p. 490
3. N.P., p. 490
4. N.P., p. 491
5. इति तु साधर्म्यवैधर्म्यधर्ममात्रविषयम् ।
   N.P., p. 491
6. त्रिविधमप्यतिदेशवाक्यागम एव ।
   N.P., p. 491
7. यत्तु श्रुतातिदेशवाक्यस्य गवयादौ अतिदेशवाक्यार्थप्रत्यभिज्ञानमुपमानं तच व्युत्पत्ति-फलमिति ।
   N.P., p. 149
8. तदप्यनुपपन्नं प्रागेव व्युत्पत्तिसिद्धेः ।
   N.P., p. 491
9. N.P., p. 491
10. एवं चानभ्युपगमे कथमिन्द्रादिशब्दव्युत्पत्तिः ? न ह्यत्र निमित्तभूतसंस्थानविशेषादिदृष्टिः ।
   N.P., p. 491

11. N.P., p. 491-2
12. तत्र, गवयगवयशब्दयोः सम्बन्धधियः प्रत्यभिज्ञाप्रत्यक्षत्वात् ।

N.D.M., p. 215

13. प्रमाणान्तरत्वे च 'सोऽयं देवदत्तः' इत्यादावपि तथात्वम् ।

N.D.M., p. 215

14. किं च 'नद्यास्तीरे फलानि' इत्यादिवाक्यगतविषयप्रत्यक्षस्यापि प्रमाणान्तरत्वम् ।

N.D.M., p. 215

15. न च 'अस्य गवयशब्दः संज्ञा' इति धीरुपमानम्, तस्य वनेचरवाक्यादवगतत्वेन स्मृतित्वात् ।

N.D.M., p. 215

16. सादृश्यं चानेकम् । तच्च सदृशानेकावयवजम् ।

N.D.M., p. 215

17. व्याप्तिग्रहणापेक्षत्वादनुमानेऽन्तर्भावः ।

Y.M.D., p. 35

18. स्मरणरूपत्वात् तस्य प्रत्यक्षेऽन्तर्भावः ।

Y.M.D., p. 34-35

19. वाक्यजन्यत्वात् शब्दे वाअन्तर्भाव ऊह्यः ।

Y.M.D., p. 35

CHAPTER 11

Dvaita Vedānta Concept Of Upamāna

The Dvaita school of Uttaramīmāṁsā, like Vaśiṣṭādvaita admits preception, inference and verbal testimony only as independent means of knowledge. The additional means accepted by other systematists are included under one or the other of these three only. The present discussion takes into consideration the account of Upamāna found in the Pramāṇa *Prakaraṇa* (one of the ten Prakaraṇas supposed to be composed by Madhva), the commentary of Jayatīrtha thereon, the *Pramāṇapaddhati* of Jayatīrtha and the *Pramāṇacandrikā* of Chalāriśeṣa. Extensive help is also sought from the commentaries of Srīrāghavendratīrtha and Śrīnivāsatīrtha on Jayatīrtha's commentary on Pramāṇaprakaraṇa also.

According to Madhva, the pramāṇa is twofold : *Kevalapramāṇa* and *Anupramāṇa*.[1] The former is the pramā itself which is sufficient for its own validity (*prāmāṇya*).[2] It has its validity through itself while the other is the conditioning process which gives rise to the former and is valid insofar as it conduces to the valid knowledge only.[3] The Anupramāṇas are three : perception, inference and testimony.[4] As regards the arthāpatti and Upamāna postulated by the other systematists as independent means of knowledge, Madhva states that they are the particular forms of inference only.[5] Jayatīrtha discusses the inclusion of Upamāna under other means of knowledge more elaborately.

As regards the view of the Mīmāṁsakas Jayatīrtha states that the Mīmāṁsakas accept three kinds of Upamāna : (i) the means of knowing similarity which the perceived object bears to the remembered object, (ii) the means of knowing the similarity which the remembered object bears to the directly perceived one and (iii) when the faultless statement leads to the knowledge of similarity. The first is exemplified thus. A person after perceiving the cow comes across a *gavaya* in the forest and remembers the cow. Then he arrives at the conclusion that the *gavaya* is similar to the cow perceived earlier. The second kind also involves the same process. The difference lies in the nature of resultant knowledge only. In this case, instead of cognising the similarity found in the directly perceived object to the remembered one, one cognises the similarity residing in the remembered object to the directly perceived one and gets the knowledge in the form that the cow is similar to the *gavaya*. In the case of the third variety, the similarity between the two objects, e.g., cow and *gavaya* is known through the authoritative statement like 'as the cow, so the *gavaya*.'[6] Jayatīrtha states that all these varieties are the cases of the perception, inference and verbal testimony respectively.[7] He shows the inclusion of the second variety in inference. The cow perceived earlier is similar to this *gavaya*, because that is the counter-relative of similarity residing in the *gavaya*, that which is the counter-relative of similarity residing in the certain object is similar to that object, as one of the twins to the other.[8]

Here, it may be argued that the similarity which serves as the probans abides in the object which is directly perceived while that serving as the probandum abides in the object remembered. How can the two similarities residing in different abodes have the relation of the probans (indicatory mark) and the possessor of that.[9] To this Jayatīrtha replies that since the invariable concomitance (*vyāpti*) is possible in the above stated manner, the difference of abode does not become a fault[10] Or, if the sameness of abode is insisted upon in two cases the above objection may be alleviated by taking the probans as—because it is counter-relative of the similarity abiding in this *gavaya*. The form of syllogism will run like this. The cow perceived earlier is similar to this *gavaya*, because the former is the counter-relative of the similarity abiding in the *gavaya*, as one of the twins to the other.[11] Here, the quality of being counter-relative of similarity abides in cow which is also the abode of similarity which is inferred. In this way, there arises no incongruity of difference of abode of the probans and its possessor (probandum).

Jayatīrtha states that the Upamāna as a means of knowledge, according to the Naiyāyikas, is the direct perception of the object meant by the name (denotation) the meaning of which is not yet cognised. The resultant cognition is the knowledge of relation of the name and the object denoted by it. The meaning conveyed by the authoritative statement is of three kinds: (i) similarity, (ii) dissimilarity and (iii) the general properties. Due to the variety of the meaning of the authoritative statement, the Upamāna is also stated to be of three kinds : (i) *sādharmyopamāna*—when the denotative relation is known with the help of the authoritative statment informing of similarity to well known object, (ii) *vaidharmyopamāna*—when the denotative relation is known with the help of the authoritative statement conveying dissimilarity to the well known object and (iii) *dharmmālropamāna*—when the denotative relation is known with the help of the authoritative statement conveying general properties of the object denoted by the term enquired.[12] They are exemplified as (i) when a person living in the city after hearing the authoritative statement from a forest-dweller 'as the cow so the *gavaya*' comes across an animal similar to the cow in the forest, he remembers the word *gavaya* and thinks that this is the animal similar to the cow told by that authoritative person.

Ultimately, he reaches the conclusion that the animal before him is the *gavaya*. (ii) After listening to a statement from the authoritative person that the horse is that which unlike cow does no have two hoofs, one comes across the horse. Then, he remembers the term horse and reaches the conclusion that the animal perceived is denoted by the term horse. (iii) After listening to a statement from some authoritative person that 'the animal which has long neck, etc., is camel', one comes across such an animal. Then, he remembers the statement and thinking that the animal has those properties concludes that it is denoted by the term camel.[13] The Upamāna of these three kinds, says Jayatīrtha, is a case of inference. The process of inference is thus. The subject of enquiry is denoted by the word *gavaya*, because itself a non-cow it is similar to cow, just as a jar by agreement in absence.[14] Rāghavendratīrtha mentions the syllogistic form of other two types of Upamāna as well. The subject of enquiry is denoted by the word horse because it has got one hoof and, thus, is dissimilar to cow.[15] The third case will be as follows. The object of denoted by the term camel because it possesses long neck, etc., just as a cow by agreement in absence.[16] Here, the upholders of Upamāna as an independent means of knowledge may argue that the forms of invariable concomitance (*vyāpti*) etc., in this case differ form those usually found in case of inference. Hence, the Upamāna should not be taken as a case of inference.[17] To this also Jayatīrtha replies that Upamāna is considered to be a particular type of inference. The types of inference are different in case of positive (*anvaya*) and the negative [*vyatireka*] type of inference but still they do not fall out of the realm of inference. Similarity, the *vyāpti* in this case also is of a particular type and thus a case of inference only.[18] Moreover, like inference, the similarity between the *vyāpti* and the *pakṣadharmatā* is required here also. Hence, it is not different from inference.[19] The above reply also alleviates the objection, if raised, regarding the acceptance of Upamāna as an independent means of knowledge on the ground of establishing a particular fact, viz., the denotative relation.[20]

Footnotes :

1. केवलमनुप्रमाणं च ।
P.P., p. 11

2. ययार्थज्ञानं केवलम् ।
P.P., p. 12

3. तत्साधनमनुप्रमाणम् ।
P.P., p. 16

4. अनुप्रमाणं त्रिविधम्—प्रयक्षमनुमानमागम इति ।
P.P., p. 31

5. अर्थापत्त्युपमे अनुमाविशेषः ।
P.P., p. 44

6. Jay. on P.P., p. 45

7. तदेतत् त्रयं क्रमेण प्रत्यक्षाद्यन्तर्भूतम् ।
Jay on P.P., p. 45

8. Jay-on P.P., p. 45
Jayatirtha puts it in simple words in his *Pramāṇapaddhati*
P. Pad., p. 17

9. P.Pad., p. 17-8

10. यो यत्सदृशः स तत्सदृशः यथा यमो यमेतरेणेति **व्याप्तिसम्भवेन** व्यधिकरणस्यादोषत्वात् ।
P.Pad., p. 18

11. एतद्द्वयगतसादृश्यप्रतियोगित्वस्य वा लिङ्गत्वेन सामानाधिकरणश्चेति ।
P.Pad., p. 18

12. Jay on P.P., p. 46

13. ibid

14. Jay. on P.P., p. 46

15. विमतः अश्वपदवाच्यः, एकशफत्वाद् गवादिविसदृशत्वात् ।
Rāghavendra on Jay. on P.P., P. 47

16. विमतः उष्ट्रपदवाच्यो दीर्घग्रीवाऽऽदिमत्त्वाद् व्यतिरेकेण गवादिवत् ।
Rāghavendra on Jay. on P.P., p. 47

17. प्रयोगप्रकारवैचित्र्यात् कथमनुमानत्वमित्यत उक्तम् ।

Jay. on P.P., p. 46

18. यथा खल्वन्वयिनो व्यतिरेकिणश्च प्रयोगप्रकारवैचित्र्येऽपि नानुमानाद्बहिर्भावः अनुमानविशेषत्वात् ।

Jay. on P.P., p. 46

19. अपेक्षितसाधर्म्यसद्भावाच्च तथाऽत्रापीति ।

Jay. on P.P., p. 46

20. एतेनोपमानस्यार्थविशेषनिष्ठतया पार्थक्यशंकाऽपि परास्ता ।

Jay. on P.P., p.46

CHAPTER 12

Śuddhādvaita Concept Of Upamāna

The Śuddhādvaita school of the Uttaramīmāṁsā also accepts only the perception, inference and the verbal testimony as the independent means of knowledge. The Upamāna is included under perception. The present discussion is based upon the *Prasthānaratnākara* of Puruṣottama which is the authoritative text of the Śuddhādvaita on logic.

As regards the view of the Naiyāyikas, Puruṣottama states that it is wrong to accept the knowledge of similarity, etc., as independent means for cognising the denotative relation.[1] The purpose of cognising the denotative relation in the cases of Upamāna postulated by the Naiyāyikas is served by the cognitive organ, like eye, in association with the remembrance of similarity which is conveyed by the authoritative statement containing the sense of similarity. If some distinct means is accepted for these cases, there would arise the undesirable contigency of admitting some distinct means for cognising the object which is perceptible but not perceived at that time.[2] Here, it will not be proper to argue that the above position will not allow the indirect *(parokṣa)* nature of Upamāna admitted by the Naiyāyikas. In fact, the Upamāna, argues Puruṣottama, is intended to be a direct means of knowledge.[3] Here, it may again be argued that the knowledge through Upamāna arises even without the operation of the senses and, hence, it should not be taken as a case of direct means of knowledge. The argument, however, is not valid. It is true that the denotative relation is cognised earlier and at the time of conforming this relation through Upamāna there is no operation of the cognitive organs, but the impression of that earlier operation of the cognitive organs still persists and there is no propriety in postulating the origin of such an experience once again.[4] Or, if the operation of the senses is insisted upon, it may be considered as a case of cognising the denotative relation like that of the words *madhukara*, etc. The similarity and the denotative relation is known through the authoritative statement and manifested at the sight of the object. Thus, the word is remembered through the impression of the similarity and it is decided at the mental level with the help of authoritative statement that the word denotes a particular object. Thus, the denotative relation is known here by mind associated with the remembrance of the sentence containing the well known word.[5] It is futher supported by the *anuvyavasāya* (perception of judgement) which ascertains the nature of the knowledge and its means through the mind and is put in the present case in the form 'I know the object as denoted by certain words'.[6]

Puruṣottama extends the application of the same argument to the Mīmāṁsā concept of Upamāna. He states that the followers of Kumārilabhaṭṭa consider the knowledge of the similarity found in the remembered object to the directly preceived one as the resultant knowledge through Upamāna just as at the sight of *gavaya* one comes to know that the cow perceived earlier is similar to the directly perceived *gavaya*.[7] This, according to Puruṣottama, is also a case of ascertainment by the mind because here also the *anuvyavasāya*, perception of judgement is in the form that the object is cognised through the mental perception.[8] Puruṣottama further criticises the Mīmāṁsakas' concept of the nature of similarity that it is the multitude of properties found in one object, different from that object. Puruṣottama objects to it that the word multitude (*bhūya*)serves no purpose because the knowledge of similarity can arise even by the single property found to be common to both the objects said to be similar.[9] In defence of the use of the word multitude the Mīmāṁsakas may argue that a single point of similarity would establish the similarity of one object to so many dissimilar objects. For example, the quality of blackness would make a mountaineer similar to a gnat. To this also Puruṣottama replies that even the insertion of the term multitude would not solve the problem in this case. We can find even some more similarities like blackness, embodied form and motion between the mountaineer and a gnat.[10] It may further be argued that similarity here indicates the same class character, uncommon to other classes, of the objects stated to be similar and not the properties only. This also states Puruṣottama leaves no necessity for the term multitude.[11] Thus, there would be the infinite regress with reference to the restriction of the multitude of properties.[12]

Footnotes :

1. सादृश्यातिदेशवाक्यार्थस्मरणसहकारेण चक्षुरादिनैव संज्ञासंज्ञिपरिच्छेदोपपत्तौ सादृश्यज्ञानादेर्मानान्तरत्वकल्पनस्यायुक्तत्वात् ।

   P.R.K., p. 148

2. अन्यथा योग्यानुपलब्धेरपि मानान्तरत्वापत्तेः ।

   P.R.K. p. 148

3. न चैवं सत्युपमितेः परोक्षत्वं व्याहन्येतेति वाच्यम् । इष्टापत्तेः ।

   P.R.K., p. 148

4. P.R.K., p. 148
5. P.R.K., p. 148
6. तदुत्तरमेतत्पदवाच्यत्वेनैनं जानामीत्यनुव्यवसायेन मानसत्वनिश्चयाच्चेति ।

   P.R.K. p. 148

7. P.R.K., p. 148-9

8. तत्रापि जानामीत्येवानुव्यवसायान्मानसत्वस्यैव निश्चयः।

P.R.K., p. 149

9. यत्तु तद्भिन्नत्वे सति तद्गतभूयोधर्मवत्त्वं सादृश्यमिति तन्न रोचिष्णु, एकेनापि सदृशबुद्धिसिद्धेर्भूयः पदस्यानतिप्रयोजनत्वात्।

P.R.K., p. 149

10. P.R.K., p. 149
11. ibid
12. तथा सति भूयस्त्वस्यापर्यवसानेऽनवस्थापत्तेः।

P.R.K., 149

CHAPTER 13

Dvaitādvaita Concept Of Upamāna

The Dvaitādvaita school of Uttaramīmāṁsā also believes in perception, inference and verbal testimony only as the independent means of knowledge.[1] The other means like implication, negation and Upamāna postulated by other systematists are included under these three only. The present discussion is based upon the *parapakṣagirivajra*—a celebrated work on Dvaitādvaita logic composed by Mādhava Mukunda.

Mādhava Mukunda discussed the details of the Mīmāṁsā view of Upamāna only. He states that the Upamāna is the knowledge of similarity and the similarity is defined as the multitude of properties which are different from the object and are found in that.[2] The Upamāna is twofold as the similarity is known through perception or scriptunal statement.[3] The first is exemplified as the face is like the moon. Here, the qualities of moon like delightfulness, etc., which are different from the moon are found in the face.[4] The example of latter type is : the unstained soul acquires the highest similarity to the Brahman. Here, the liberated soul which is stated to be different from Brahman acquires the properties of consciousness and omniscience found in the Brahman.[5] Thus, what Mukunda seems to mean is that the means of knowing the similarity is not some independent one but the perception and the valid testimony only. Hence, the Upamāna is included in the perceptioin when the similarity is known through perception and in the valid testimony when the similarity is known through scriptural statements. The similarity conveyed through the latter means cannot be tested on the basis of our common experience. The view recorded by Mādhava Makunda is unique because the Mīmāṁsakas, unlike the above record do not lay equal stress upon both the perception of similarity and the authoritative statement.

Casually it may also be remarked here that Mādhava Mukunda was also aware of the division of Upamāna into three—sādharmyopamāna, vaidharmyopamāna and the *dharmamātropamāna* as he refutes the application of the three kinds of Upamāna in the case of the knowledge of Brahman.[6] However, it seems that he does not show the way of inclusion of all these varieties under perception and verbal testimony in details because like similarity the dissimilarity and the description of the general properties also may have their source either in perception or authoritative statement and, hence, become the case of these two means of knowledge only.

As regards the Nyāya concept of Upamāna Mādhava Mukunda makes a simple remark that the Upamāna envisaged by them is included under instance which forms a component of a syllogism in inference.[7]

Footnote :

1. वस्तुतस्तु प्रत्यक्षानुमानशब्दाख्यानि त्रीण्येव प्रमाणानि ।
P.P.G.V., p. 254
2. सादृश्यज्ञानमुपमानं सादृश्यं च तद्भिन्नत्वे सति तद्गतभूयोधर्मवत्त्वं तद्विषयकं ज्ञान-मुपमानमित्यर्थः ।
P.P.G.V., p. 218
3. तच्च द्विविधं प्रत्यक्षमूलं श्रुतिमूलं चेति ।
P.P.G.V., p. 218
4. P.P.C.V., p. 218-19
5. P.P.G.V., p. 219
6. P.P.G.V., p. 260-61
7. उपमानस्य दृष्टान्तमात्रैकविग्रहत्वेनानुमानावयव उदाहरणेऽन्तर्भावः ।
P.P.G.V., p. 254

CHAPTER 14

Resumé

In the foregoing pages a detailed and critical account of various problems regarding Upamāna as found in the works of the certain outstanding authors was given.

Here follows a brief retrospect of the whole in its essentials. Upamāna is accepted as an independent means of knowledge in the system of Nyāya, the Pārvamīmāṁsā and the Advaita school of Uttaramīmāṁsā. However, we find that the conception of these systems do not coincide in respect of the details of Upamāna. The Naiyāyikas are on one side and the Pūrvamīmāṁsakas and the Advaita Vedāntins are on the other. Their main difference is regarding the nature of the resultant knowledge through Upamāna. According to the Naiyāyikas it refers to the denotative relation between the word and the object of a certain class, while according to the Pūrvamīmāṁsakas and the Advaita Vedāntins it refers to the similarity which the remembered object bears to the directly perceived one. It further leads to the difference regarding the object of Upamāna which is the denotative relation according to the Naiyāyikas, and the remembered object qualified by similarity according to the Pūrvamīmāṁsakas and the Advaita Vedāntins. Moreover, the Naiyāyikas lay more stress on the authoritative statement while the Mīmāṁsakas do not take it as essential for Upamāna. The purpose or the practical utility of Upamāna held by the Pūrvamīmāṁsakas may not be acceptable to the Adaita Vedānta. The Pūrvamīmāṁsakas hold that Upamāna helps in replacing one object by the other similar to it in the context of the sacrificial rites. It would, however, not be consistent with the spirit of Advaita Vedānta. The Advaita Vedāntins would accept Upamāna for the purpose of explaining super natural experience on the analogy of the common worldly experience, i.e., to explain the unobserved fact through its similarity to the observed one. Between the Prābhākara and the Bhāṭṭa school of the Pūrvamīmāṁsā also there is a difference regarding the nature of similarity. The Prābhākaras unlike the Bhāṭṭa consider similarity as a distinct category. We do not come across such a means of knowledge in Western philosophy also. The Western philosophy accepts analogy as source of knowledge but the nature of analogy is quite different from that of Upamāna.Analogy is a from of argument through which some further resemblance is inferred in some other object from a resemblance between two known aspects. Hence, it cannot be identical with Upamāna.

As regards the Nyāya definition of Upamāna Gautama states that Upamāna is the means of cognising some unknown object through its similarity to the known one. From the wording of the *sūtra* it is not clear whether the unknown object here refers to the denotative relation as understood by his commentators or same other object itself. The latter alternative seems to be preferable. The means are the similarity and the authoritative statement conveying it. Upamāna does not depend upon the degree in similarity. The only condition is that the similarity should be well known Vātsyāyana considers the authoritative statement 'as the cow so the *gavaya*' as Upamāna. He makes an explicit mention of the resultant knowledge as the relation of the name with the corresponding object. Vātsyāyana further clarifies his position by offering two more examples of Upamāna as the *Mudgaparṇī* is like *Mudga* and *Māṣaparṇī* is like *māṣa*. Like Vātsyāyana Uddyotakara also holds that the resultant knowledge refers to the denotative relation. Uddyotakara, however, differs from Vātsyāyana regarding the means of cognition. He considers perception of similarity associated with the revival of the impressions caused by the authoritative statement as the means of Upamāna. He makes further innovation by introducing the element of dissimilarity as the basis of Upamāna. Vācaspati understands Upamāna as *Pramāṇa* strictly in the sense of *Karaṇa* (means). He adds that the term *sādharmya* is used elliptically for the properties in general and as such the *upamiti* can be derived through the unique characteristics also. Jayantabhaṭṭa takes into account the views of his predecessors under two heads: the earlier and the contemporary. He records the definition offered by Vātsyāyana under the earlier head and that by Uddyotakara under the latter. He alleviates the objections levelled against both the views.

Thus, Gautama and Vātsyāyana regarded Upamāna as of one kind, only i.e., based on similarity. Uddyotakara introduces dissimilarirty as the basis of Upamāna and it comes to be of two kinds. Vācaspati further introduces the statement of characteristics in general also as a basis Upamāna and, thus, it comes to be of three kinds. The latter texts of Nyāya maintain that Upamāna is of three kinds (i) *sādharmyopamāna* i.e. Upamāna through similarity, (ii) *vaidhamyopamāna* i.e. Upamāna through dissimilarity and (iii) *dharmamātropamāna* i.e. Upamāna through mere properties.

Gautama's definition of Upamāna leaves the purpose or the utility of Upamāna unexplained. According to Diṅnāga, Gautama accepts Upamāna to cognise the similarity which the *gavaya* bears to the cow or to cognise the *gavaya* as qualified by the similarity to the cow. Vātsyāyana, for the first time, clarifies the idea of practical utility of Upamāna that it helps to collect the medicinal herbs like *Māṣaparṇī* and *Mudgaparṇī*.

Jayantabhaṭṭa adds that Upamāna has unique part to play in the performance of vedic rite which enjoins the killing of a *gavaya*. He further adds though it has no bearing upon final emancipation like the other three means of knowledge, yet Upamāna helps in acquiring the knowledge of the objects to be known. Gautama has discussed Upamāna to render this useful service to all.

The Naiyāyikas spare no pain to establish Upamāna as a distinct means of knowledge. Gautama negates the inferential nature of Upamāna on the ground that the earlier, unlike the latter, does not lead to the knowledge of unperceived object through perceived one. Moreover, Upamāna unlike inference is always expressed in the form 'as..., so...' Vātsyāyana further adds that Upamāna is always for the sake of another person only while inference is for one's own benefit also. Jayantabhaṭṭa further adds that Upamāna, unlike inference, does not depend upon invariable concomitance. Udayana refutes many arguments possible to be raised in favour of including Upamāna under inference. He maintains that the syllogism cannot be formed as the word *gavaya* denotes the animal *gavaya* because it is applied to the latter by cultured people without taking recourse to some function of word other than direct denotation just as the word *go* used in the sense of cow denotes a cow. The probans here is vitiated by the fallacy of nonestablishment of the reason. To deduce such a relation on the basis of taking the authoritative statement as *vyāpti* would again be based upon the wrong interpretation of the authoritative statement. Ānandapūrṇa and Śaṁkaramiśra try to include Upamāna under inference on the ground of the syllogism which is already proved to be defective by Udayana. Jayatīrha however, puts the syllogism in a different form : the subject of enquiry is denoted by the word *gavaya* because itself a non cow it is similar to a cow, just as a jar by agreement in absence.

Upamāna cannot be included under verbal testimony also. Most of the critics of Upamāna argue that Upamāna envisaged by Vātsyāyana is a case of verbal testimony. Uddyotakara refutes the view of Diṅnāga in this connection. Vācaspati holds that the authoritative statement conveys that the object denoted is different from the objects of its own class and those of other classes and as such it cannot lead you to the denotative relation which requires the knowledge of the genus which in turn cannot be acquired merely through the authoritative statement. Jayantabhaṭṭa further adds that the totality of causal conditions are not the same in case of Upamāna and verbal testimony. The verbal testimony operates through verbal understanding or the validity the knowledge of speaker while Upamāna requires well known similarity in addition. Moreover, unlike verbal testimony the object is not present at the time of hearing the statement itself. Even if the rational doubts about the contents of knowledge are not satisfied and Upamāna is considered to be a case of verbal testimony, it would be a case of doubtful knowledge because we have no faith in the veracity of the statement. Udayana adds if Upamāna would be a case of verbal testimony, the knowledge in this case would be admitted as arising in a person who has heard the authoritative statement but has not yet seen the *gavaya*. Moreover, the similarity to the cow conveyed through the authoritative statement is not a cause of restricting the usage to the word *gavaya* in the sense of animal *gavaya*. The Upamāna cannot be the result of the combination of perception and verbal testimony also. Here, perception and verbal testimony take place at deferent times while the objects producing the effect together should operate at the same time. Otherwise, inference and verbal testimony would also be the cases of perception only. The causes of inference and verbal testimony, viz., *lingaparāmarśa* and words are the result of perception.

The Naiyāyikas further try to disprove the inclusion of Upamāna under remembrance on the ground that the denotative relation cannot be known through the authoritative statement only and as such it cannot be considered to be cognised earlier to the perception of the cow. Thus, it cannot be a case of remembrance pure and simple. As a matter of fact, the critics are right to say that the elements of Upamāna can be explained through one or the other means of knowledge. They ignore the combined process which involves novelty in the activity of mind and, hence, makes the Upamāna an independent means of knowledge.

The Pūrvamīmāṁsakas also accept Upamāna as an independent means of knowledge. The view of the Pūrvamīmāṁsakas, however, differ from that of the Naiyāyikas. There is only a minor difference between the views of the Prābhākara and Bhāṭṭa school of the Pūrvamīmāṁsā. Prābhākaras, unlike the Bhāṭṭas consider similarity as an independent category.

Śabara's definition of Upamāna implies that the similarity is the *karaṇa* and the remembered object is the object. Śabara takes recourse to the stock example of the Mīmāṁsakas and states that here the *karaṇa* is the *gavayadarśana* (perception of the *gavaya)* and the resultant knowledge refers to *gosmaraṇa* (remembrance of the cow). To reconcile the example of *karaṇa* the term *gavayadarśana* should be understood in the sense of the perception of *gavaya* qualified by its similarity to the cow. The result of the Upamāna is said to be the cognition of the object not in contact with the senses and is illustrated as the remembrance of the cow. The nature of the definition and that of the illustration do not correspond. *G. P. Bhāṭṭa's* attempt to reconcile the two does not satisfy. Here, it may be suggested that the term *gosmaraṇa* should be interpreted in the sense of the remembrance of the cow as qualified by its similarity to the *gavaya*. The object of Upamāna is this sort of remembrance only. Kumārilabhaṭṭa explicitly states that the result of Upamāna is the cognition of a thing remembered as qualified by its similarity to the perceived object or the similarity as qualified by previously known object. Thus, all the authors of the Pūrvamīmāṁsā agree that in the stock example of Upamāna the means is the similarity which the *gavaya* bears to the cow and the resultant knowledge refers to the similarity which the cow bears to the *gavaya*. The term *gosmaraṇa* in the definition of Upamāna offered by Śabara is interpreted in a different way by Prabhākara, but still he does not go against the interpretation of the statement as a whole offered by the Bhaṭṭa school. Prabhākara understands the meaning of the term as in the case of a person who has already seen a cow. Though there remains nothing to correspond to the resultant knowledge, yet the explanation offered by Śālikanātha implies that the resultant knowledge refers to the cow. As regards the practical utility of Upamāna Kumārilabhaṭṭa states that it helps us to get the knowledge of the sacrificial details in case of rite in connection of which the details are to be taken from some other rite. For example, some details not given in the *Saurya* sacrifice are known as the same as mentioned in the case of *Āgneya* sacrifice through Upamāna because of their having a common deity. Similarily, the purpose of *vrīhi* can be served by *nīvāra* because of their similarity, to each other. Thus, similarity plays a major role in the concept of Upamāna held by the Pūrvamīmāṁsā. Kumārilabhaṭṭa strongly advocates for similarity as a positive entity. His definition of similarity has been resorted to by almost all the critics of the Mīmāṁsā concept of Upamāna. He defines similarity as the presence in one class of objects of such an arrangement of the constituent parts as in common to other class of objects. Pārthasārathi adds that the term common parts suggests the similarity in respect of the properties and activities as well. The similarity seems to be of various kinds as it rests upon birth, property, substance, action, power and the specific character. In case of the similar objects one or more of these are found to be common. Kumārilabhaṭṭa further clarifies that similarity being an inherent relation does not rest upon these properties but in their locus. Thus, similarity should not be confused with the properties themselves. The similarity is neither absolutely eternal nor subjected to utter annihilation. It is subjected to destruction as it resides in an individual which is subject to destruction but the similarity like class inheres in all individual objects of the class and since no class is subjected to utter destruction, the similarity is also eternal. The similarity is not identical with the class also. Nor is it necessary that the similarity exists in the object of one class only. The cow and the *gavaya* belong to different classes but are similar to each other. The perception of the similarity residing in the perceived object immediately gives rise to the knowledge of similarity.

Prabhākara tries to establish that similarity is a distinct category. This is further supported by Śālikanātha arguing that the existence of similarity can be established through our common behaviour. Moreover, it cannot be included in any of the categories of the Vaiśeṣikas. The view, however, is strongly criticised. The view cannot account for the cause of differentiation into great and small degree in similarity. The upholders of similarity as an independent category cannot explain the nature of similarity. Again it involves the incongruity about its exact location as well. Further, the similarity as an independent category cannot be specified as eternal or non-eternal. Hence, it is not regarded as an independent category at all.

The Mīmāṁsakas have also tried their best to prove Upamāna as a distinct means of knowledge. The view has met scathing criticism at the hands of its opponents. The main arguments in this direction are based upon the ground that the knowledge arrived at through Upamāna can be attained through some other means of knowledge and hence, there is no need of accepting Upamāna as an independent means of knowledge.

Jayanta argues here that the practical utility of Upamāna can be served by remembrance. As such, it will be a case of remembrance and thus will not bring out the efficacy of Upamāna. Even if it is accepted as different from remembrance, it can very well be a case of inference. Udayana also argues that no object requires particularly the Upamāna for its cognition. If the Upamāna is thought to be necessary for cognising similarity, the dissimilarity would also be cognised through Upamāna. The Sāṁkhyas find no purpose of postulating Upamāna as an independent means of knowledge. The similarity supposed to be cognised through Upamāna is cognised through perception. Śāntarakṣita also finds no object to be cognised specially through Upamāna. If the Mīmāṁsakas insist that the Upamāna should be accepted for cognising similarity, the dissimilarity would also require independent means of cognition. Moreover, if a slight element of means of knowledge as found in Upamāna is considered to be enough for a distinct means of knowledge, there will arise the undesirable contingency of accepting infinite means of knowledge because such a slight element of valid means of knowledge is found in various modes. The Jaina logicians also criticise the independent status of Upamāna mainly on the ground that such a position will require the postulation of some independent means for cognising dissimilarity. Veṅkaṭanātha also rejects the independent status of Upamāna on the same ground. The followers of Dvaita, the Śuddhādvaita and the Dvaitādvaita school of Uttaramīmāṁsā also do not find the need of accepting of Upamāna as an indipendent means of knowledge. That is why the other systematists include Upamāna under some other means of knowledge. Bhāsarvajña, Jayantabhaṭṭa, Śrīdhara and Śāntarakṣita include it under remembrance. Udayana considers it a case of presumption and hence, finally includes it under inference. Vācaspati includes it under perception, the Jainas under recognition, Veṅkaṭanātha under remembrance or inference, Jayatīrtha under any of perception, inference and verbal testimony, Puruṣottama under mental perception and Mukunda Mādhava under perception or valid testimony. The Mīmāṁsakas, however, reject any of these possiblitlies. The Upamāna cannot be case of perception. The object of Upamāna may be considered as either the similarity which the remembered object bears to the directly perceived one or the remembered object qualified by its similarity to the directly perceived one. Neither of these, however, can be the object of Perception. Some systematists like Udayana, Jayantabhaṭṭa, Mādhva and Jayatīrtha favour to include the Upamāna under inference. Their main argument is that the knowledge arising through Upamāna can be acquired through syllogism and as such there is no need of postulating Upamāna as an independent means of knowledge. Moreover, it would involve the undesirable contingency of admitting some other means of knowledge for the cognition of dissimilarity which arises through the same process but differs in respect of contents. The Mīmāṁsakas, however, are not prepared to leave the ground. They strongly refute the above contention. Kumārila argues that the conditions, viz., a faultless *vyāpti* and *pakṣadharmatā* are not essential for the process in Upamāna. Pārthasārthi further explains that the form of syllogism would lead to the erroneous conclusion. The Upamāna when reduced to syllogism will have three steps : (i) perception of similarity with (ii) the directly perceived object, and (iii)the resultant knowledge. If the first is held to be a probans, it would lead to the wrong supposition that the first step leads to the third directly. The Upamāna again lacks some of the technicalities of inference. Unlike inference, the factor of the earlier knowledge of non-conditioned invariable concomitance is not necessary in case of Upamāna. Moreover, unlike the probans in inference the supposed probans in Upamāna does not require its absence in the dissimilar objects. The probans and the probandum occur at the same place. The causal condition leading to inference are different from those leading to Upamāna. Inference is based upon the remembrance of the rule or the nature of relation between the probans and the probandum but in the case of Upamāna such a relation is not ascertained earlier. The theory of the Mīmāṁsakas has met scathing criticism on some other points as well. Jayanta states that the nature of the knowledge attained through Upamāna lacks the support of our common experience. In the stock example of the Mīmāṁsakas, at the sight of the *gavaya* what generally comes to one's mind is that the directly perceived cow is similar to the remembered cow and not vice versa. Jayanta criticises the Mīmāṁsā view of the practical utility of Upamāna also. The definition of Upamāna does not correspond to their example to suggest the practical utility of Upamāna. Moreover, the Upamāna cannot held in transforming the minor details of one sacrifice to the other because it cannot play the role of scriptures. The arguments, however, do not stand the test of reasoning. When a person gives importance to a certain thing and comes across some other thing similar to it, he would surely remember the former. If the Upamāna is considered to be a means of cognising similarity which the remembered object bears to the directly perceived one, there is no harm in accepting that the dissimilarity which the remembered object bears to the directly perceived one is also cognised through Upamāna. The Mīmāṁsakas, however, think that dissimilarity means the absence of similarity and as such should not be considered as cognised positively. This is, however, not convincing. Dissimilarity should not be understood as merely the negation of similarity but an independent object of cognition.

The followers of the Advaita school of the Uttara-Mīmāṁsā also admit Upamāna as an independent means of knowledge. The concept of the Advaita Vedāntins does not essentially differ from the view of the Pūrvamīmāṁsakas.

Ānandapūrṇa also tries his best to establish that Upamāna is an independent means of knowledge. It cannot be a case of perception for the knowledge of the cow as qualified by similarity to *gavaya* cannot be attained through the sense-object contact. Ānandapūrṇa further rejects the view of the supporter of Upamāna under inference mainly on the ground that they do not put forth a faultless syllogistic form. Dharmarāja Adhvaryu observes that in our common behaviour no one is actually seen to deduce such a knowledge of similarity through inference. Moreover, the *anuvyavasāya* also does not go in favour of the inclusion of Upamāna under inference. Ānandapūrṇa further rejects the possibility of inclusion of Upamāna under remembrance by criticising the argument adduced by Śrīdhara and Bhāsavajña to include Upamāna under remembrance. He puts forth some additional reasons also to establish the difference between remembrance and Upamāna. Ānandapūrṇa further tries to prove that the Upamāna cannot be a case of presumption also. The supporters of the inclusion of Upamāna under presumption argue that the cognition of *gavaya* as similar to cow would imply that the cow is also similar to *gavaya*. The reasoning, however, involves the undesirable contingency of the inclusion of Upamāna under remembrance. Moreover, presumption is based upon invariable concomitance and hence, cannot include Upamāna under it. The opponents take the help of the example of the cognition of the size to prove the case. Ānandapūrṇa, however, suggests that the example does not fit in the context of the knowledge of similarity. Ānandapūrṇa further tries to prove that the acceptance of Upamāna does not involve the undesirable contingency of the acceptance of some other means for cognising dissimilarity. The argument of Ānandapūrṇa, however, is based upon the fact of taking dissimilarity as an absence of similarity and, hence, is not satisfactory. Ānandapūrṇa further tries to prove that similarity is an independent positive entity mainly on the ground that the position cannot be rejected through any means of knowledge. Thus, the Advaita views of Upamāna is like that of the Pūrvamīmāṁsā. The purpose of Upamāna considered by the Pūrvamīmāṁsā will not be acceptable to the Advaita Vedāntins. The Vedāntins do not attach importance to the ritualistic practices and hence, the sole purpose of Upamāna, according to them, will not be the replacing of one object with the other similar to it. Therefore, the Vedāntins would accept Upamāna for explaining the passages speaking of super natural experience of reality which reminds the experience of the common life.

A study of the views of the critics of Upamāna reveals that except the Cārvākas and a few other philosophers who reduce it to the non-valid source of knowledge like *smṛti* no thinker rejects the validity of the process of Upamāna as leading to the valid knowledge. They, however, reject the independent status to Upamāna as a means of knowledge. They are in favour of including it under some of the other means of knowledge accepted by them. The critics are also not unanimous in including it under the other means of knowledge. The difference is prompted mainly by the stress on different elements of Upamāna. That is why different systematists include it under different means of knowledge. Since there is a great difference between the Nyāya and the Mīmāṁsā schools, both the views are included under different means even by a single school. As regards the Nyāya view, Bhāsarvajña includes it under verbal testimony. The Vaiśeṣikas favour its inclusion under inference. Amongst the Sāṁkhyas, the Yuktidīpikā includes it under verbal testimony, Vācaspati under verbal testimony or inference, Gauḍapāda under verbal testimony, the Jayamṅagalā under verbal testimony or inference and Māṭhara, the Sāṃkhyacandrikā and Vijñānbhikṣu under inference. Amongst the Buddhists, Diṅnāga includes it under perception or verbal testimony, Śantarakṣita under memory or inference. The Jaina logicians include it under recognition. Amongst the Uttaramīmāṁsakas, Vedāntadeśika favours its inclusion under verbal testimony, Meghanādasūri under recognition, Śrīnivāsadāsa under any of the perception, inference or verbal testimony and Jayatīrtha under perception. As regards the Pūrvamīmāṁsa view, Bhāsarvajña and Jayantabhaṭṭa include it under remembrance. Amongst the Vaiśeṣikas, Udayana includes it under inference and Śrīdhara under remembrance. The Sāṁkhyas include it under preception and the Buddhists under remembrance. The Jaina logicians include it under recognition. Amongst the Uttaramīmāṁsakas, Veṅkaṭnātha includes it under remembrance or inference, Jayatīrtha under perception or inference or verbal testimony, Puruṣottama, under mental perception, and Mukunda Mādhava reduces it to eihter of the perception and valid testimony.

As a matter of fact, the difference regarding the acceptance or rejection of Upamāna as an independent means of knowledge seems to be rooted in the presupposition of different systematists with regard to the differences regarding the factors determining the means of knowledge. In the system of the Bauddhas the number of the means of knowledge is determined by the types of the objects to be known. The objects to be known are of two types : unique particular *(svalakṣaṇa)* and universal (*sāmānyalakṣaṇa*). Both of these are cognised through perception and inference and there arises no need for admitting Upamāna. The Sāṁkhyas also hold that the number of the means of knowledge is determined by the nature of the objects to be known and since all the objects can be cognised through three means only, they do not need Upamāna as a distinct means. The Mīmāṁsakas determine the number of means of knowledge through the types of the causal aggergate of knowledge. The Upamāna requires different causal aggregate and is therefore, admitted to be a distinct means of knowledge. In theory of the Naiyāyikas the number of the means of knowledge is determined by the nature of causal aggregate of knowledge and the nature of the resultant knowledge. These are different from other means in case of Upamāna. Hence, it is regarded as an independent means of knowledge. According to Jainas the number of the means of knowledge is determined by the nature of the resultant knowledge and, hence, they include Upamāna under recognition.

Selected Bibliography

Aṣṭasāhasrī, Bombay, 1915.

Bauddhatarkabhāṣā, Baroda, 1942.

Bṛhatī, (with Ṛjuvimalāpañcīkā), Madras, 1934.

Gauḍapādabhāṣya, (with Sāṁkhyakārikā) Poona, 1972.

Jayamaṅgalā, (with Sāṁkhyakārikā) Varanasi, 1970.

Kāśikā, (with Ślokavārttika), 3 parts, Trivandrum Sanskrit Series No. XV, XCIV, CL.

Kiraṇāvalī (with Praśastapādabhāṣya), Baroda, 1971.

Mānameyodaya, Madras, 1933.

Māṭharavṛtri, (with Sāṁkhyakārikā), Varanasi, 1970.

Nayadyumaṇiḥ, Madras, 1956.

Nyāyabinduṭīkā Meerut, 1975.

Nyāyabhāṣya, (with Nyāyasūtras) Benaras, 1925.

Nyāyachandrikā (with Nyāyaprakāśikā), Madras, 1959.

Nyāyakandalī (with Praśastapādabhāṣya), Varansi, 1977.

Nyāyakusumāñjali, Darbhanga, 1972.

Nyāyamañjarī, Varansi, 1971.

Nyāyamañjarīgranthibhaṅga, Ahmedabad, 1972.

Nyāyapariśuddhi, Varansi 1918.

Nyāyasāra, Poona, 1922.

Nyāyasiddhāntamañjarī, Varanasi, 1916.

Nyāyasiddhāntamuktāvali,	(with Dinakarī and Rāmarudrī), Varanasi, 1972.
Nyāyavārttika,	Benaras, 1916.
Nyāyavārttikatātparyaṭīkā,	2 parts, Benaras, 188.
Nyāyavārttikavṛtti,	Bombay, 1949.
Parapakṣagirivajra,	Vrindavan, 1959.
Prakaraṇapañcikā,	Benaras, 1961.
Pramāṇanayatattvāloka	Beyaver, 1942.
Pramāṇapaddhati	Bombay, 1896.
Pramāṇaprakaraṇa	(one of the ten prakaraṇas written by Madhva), Mardas, 1969. Varanasi, 1968.
Pramāṇavārttika	Bombay, 1941.
Praśastapādabhāṣya	(with Kiraṇāvalī), Baroda, 1971.
Prasthānaratnākara	Benaras, 1909.
Śābarabhāṣya	Poona, 1929.
Sāṁkhyacandrikā	(with Sāṁkhyakārikā), Benaras, 1971.
Sāṃkhyakārikā	(with Gauḍapādabhāṣya), Poona, 1972.
Sāṁkhyapravacanabhāṣya	Calcutta, 1936.
Sāṁkhyatattvakaumudī	Poona, 1965.
Sāstradīpikā	Benaras, 1913.
Ślokavārttika,	(with Nyāyaratnākara),Varanasi, 1978. (with Umveka's Commentary) Madras, 1971.
Śrutyantakalpavalli	Benares, 1927.
Tarkabhāṣā of Yaśovijaya	Delhi, 1973.
Tarkasaṁgraha	Poona, 1963.
Tārkikarakṣā	Benaras, 1960.
Tattvasaṁgaraha	(with Pañcikā), Varanasi, 1968.
Vaiśeṣikasūtropaskāra	Benaras, 1969.

Vedāntaparibhāṣā	Varanasi, 1967.
Yatīndramatadīpikā	Madras, 1967.
Yuktidīpika,	Delhi, 1967.
Yogasūtra,	(with Vyāsabhāṣya, Tattvavaiśāradī, and Yogavārttika), Varanasi, 1971.
Bhatt, Govardhan P.	Epistemology of the Bhāṭṭa School of Pūrvamīmāṁsā, Benaras 1962.
Bijalwan, C.D.	Indian theory of Knowledge, Delhi, 1977.
Bothra, Puspa	The Jaina theory of Perception, Delhi, 1976.
Chatterjee, S.C.	Nyāya theory of knowledge, Culcutta, 1950.
Datta, D.M.	Six Ways of Knowing, Culcutta,
Jwala Prasad	1972. History of Indian Epistemology, Delhi, 1958.
Randle, H.N.	Fragments from Diṅnāga, London, 1926.
Shastri, Kailash Chandra	Jaina Nyāya, Varanasi, 1966.
Sukhalalji.	Advanced Studies in Indian Logic and Metaphysics, Calcutta, 1961.
Tripathi, C.L.	Problem of knowledge in Yogācāra Buddhism, Varanasi, 1972.
Vidyabhuṡan S. C.	History of Indian Logic, Calcutta, 1921

INDEX

adhyavasāya, 5
Advaita
Vedānta, 4, 6, 12, 29, 44, 98, 99, 109 147, 157-8
āgama, 1, 36, 129,
arthya, 12
Akalaṅka, 6,34
analogy, 148
Ānandapūraṇa, 29, 30, 44, 87, 98-109, 150
anubhūti, 6
anupalabdhi, 12
anuparmāṇa, 137
anuvyavasāya, 33, 41, 50, 79, 101, 143, 157
Anuyogadvārasūtra, 129
anvaya, 141
anvayī, 46
apramā, 5
arthāpatti,12, 106, 117
asiddhatva, 48
Aṣṭasāhasri, 6n
Ātman, 7
authoritative statement, 13, 22, 26-33, 35, 37, 39, 40, 42, 43, 45, 47-50, 52-60 67, 107, 133-136, 140, 142, 143, 146-148, 150-1
Aviddhakaraṇa, 59, 126
avidyā, 5
avīta, 119
Bauddhas, 3, 7, 159
Bhāsarvajña,36, 37, 50, 61, 71, 78, 80, 81, 85, 101, 111- 113, 155, 157-159
Bṛhatī, 64, 66n, 70, 93n, 94n
buddhi, 7, 11
Buddhists, 12, 33, 159
Cārvāka, 12, 24, 25, 158
Chalāriśeṣa 137
cuta, 11
cittavṛtti, 5, 11
corroborative instance, 127
denotative relation. 13, 20, 29, 32, 34, 38, 40, 46, 54, 56,111,112, 115, 118, 125-130, 131, 133, 135, 141-143, 147, 148, 150, 151
dhārāvāhika jñāna, 21, 23, 140, 146, 149
Dharmarāja Adhvaryu, 4, 6, 98, 99, 100, 101, 157
Dinkarī,23n
Diṅnāga, 23, 33, 39, 41, 52-54, 123, 150,158
Dvaita Vedānta, 4, 12, 32, 137, 155
Dvaitādvaita Vedānta, 4, 12, 33, 78, 145, 155
Gauḍapāda, 38, 52, 122, 158
Gauḍapādabhāṣya, 38n, 52n,122n
Gautama, 13-15, 21, 23-25, 36, 41, 46, 54, 112, 141, 149
Hemacandra, 34n, 130n, 131,131n
hetu, 68
hetvābhāsa,90
illusion, 9
implication, 63, 88

inference, 8, 12, 14, 17, 25, 27, 30-33, 35-39, 42-47, 49, 50,
52, 55, 57, 62, 63, 70, 75, 78, 79, 87, 92, 94, 100, 109, 112
114, 115, 117, 119, 121, 122, 127, 129, 132, 133, 135, 137,
138, 140-142,145, 150, 151, 154-56, 158, 159
inherence, 72, 84, 105
inherent. 101, 107
inveriable concomitance, 8, 31, 45, 48, 49, 89-91, 93, 107, 141, 150, 156
Jaimini, 63
Jaina, 5-8, 34, 39, 58, 77, 78, 129, 155, 158, 159
Jayamaṅgalā, 38, 38n, 44, 45n, 52, 52n, 122, 122n, 158,
Jayantabhaṭṭa,9, 10, 20, 21, 23, 42, 48 55, 78, 80, 81, 86, 88, 95-97, 149, 150, 154-56, 159
Jayatīrtha, 32, 32n, 39, 39n, 45, 45n, 78, 79n, 89, 89n, 90, 137, 138, 138n, 139, 140, 140n, 141, 141n, 150, 155, 159,
jñāna, 2
Kamalaśīla, 3
Karaṇa, 7-10, 16, 18, 35, 37, 39, 42, 149, 152,
kevalapramāṇa, 137
kevalavyatireki, 50
Kiraṇāvalī, 38, 38n, 51n, 75n, 78n, 87n, 114n, 115, 116n, 117n,
Kumārilabhaṭṭa, 25-28, 39, 40, 53, 57, 61, 63-65, 67, 68, 80, 85 86, 90-92, 99, 143, 152, 153, 155
Laghīyastraya, 34n, 130n, 131n
Liberation
Liṅga, 8
liṅgaparāmarśa,58, 151
logic, 1
Mādhava Mukunda, 33, 79, 145, 146, 155
Madhva, 37, 88
Mānameyodaya,28n, 29n, 56n, 60n, 66n, 71n, 72n
Māṭhara, 38, 44, 122, 158
Māṭharavṛtti, 38n, 44n, 122n
Meghanādārisūri, 31, 32, 58, 132, 134, 158
memory, 39, 62, 64, 74, 75, 96
mental perception, 144, 155, 159, 151
metaphysics, 1
Nīmāṁsā,63, 74, 77-79, 88, 95, 96, 101, 113, 116, 121, 129, 132, 143, 145, 153, 158
Mīmāṁsakas, 6-8, 74-77, 79, 87, 89, 90, 94, 95, 97, 111-114, 117, 118, 122, 130, 138, 144, 146, 152, 154-156, 159
Mīmāṃsāsūtra, 63
Mokṣa,2
Mokṣākargupta, 34, 61, 73, 125, 128
Naiyāyikas, 3, 5-9, 12, 21, 23-25, 27-29, 31, 32, 35-37, 40, 41, 43, 46, 56, 58-60, 62, 70, 88, 111, 114, 119, 121-123, 126, 127, 130-133, 139, 142, 147, 149, 159
Nārāyaṇa, 28, 71, 72, 97
Nayadyumaṇī, 31n, 58n, 132, 135n,
negation, 76, 124,
nirvikalpa, 81, 85, 105, 113
Nyāya, 1, 2, 13, 27, 33, 34,36, 38, 44, 61, 96, 115,

121,125- 127, 129, 130, 139, 146-148, 158
Nyāyabhāṣya, 2, 51, 16n, 17n, 23n, 47n
Nyayabinduṭikā, 3n
Nyāyacandrikā, 30n, 44n, 87n, 98n, 99n, 100n, 101n, 102, 103, 105n-109n
Nyāyakandalī, 5n, 36n, 38, 40n, 42, 51n, 75n, 78n, 84n, 85n, 87n, 114n, 115n, 116n-118n
Nyāyakusumāñjali, 42n, 48n, 50n, 57n, 58
Nyāyamañjarī, 8n, 9n, 10n, 21n, 24n, 42n, 55n, 56n, 74n, 75n, 78n, 81n, 82, 86n, 88n, 95n, 96n
Nyāyapariśuddhi, 4n, 30n, 31n, 39n, 52n, 53n, 78n, 84n, 88n, 132, 133n 134
Nayāyaratnākara, 27n, 40n, 69n
Nyāyasāra, 36n-38n, 57n, 78n, 81n, 85n, 111, 112n, 113n
Nyāyasārasaṁgraha, 22n, 23n
Nyāyasiddhāntamanjari, 23n
Nayāyasiddhāntamuktavalī, 50n
Nyāyasūtra, 14n, 15n, 24n, 25n, 47n, 111, 131
Nyāyavārttika, 15n, 17n, 18n, 19n, 23n, 25, 33n, 39n, 41n, 42n, 52n, 53n, 54n, 54n, 123n
Nyāyavārttikatātparyaṭīkā, 18n-20n, 23n, 39n, 41n, 42n, 52n-54n, 123n
Nyāyavārttikatātparyaṭīkāpariśuddhi, 72n, 73n,
Nyāyavatārvārttikavṛtti, 6n
nāda, 58
pakṣa, 46, 88, 90, 91
pakṣadharmatā, 32, 46, 90, 141, 155
Pañcikā, 64n, 66n, 70n, 71n, 94n, 95n, 127n
parāmarśa, 9
Parapakṣagirivajra, 33n, 79n, 145, 145n, 146
parokṣa, 129, 142
Pārthasārathimiśra, 4, 26, 27, 65, 68, 69, 153, 155
Patañjali, 10
Paurāṇikas, 12
perception, 8, 10, 12, 14, 18, 26-28, 31, 33 39, 42, 56-58, 61- 66, 73 78-80, 89, 99, 104, 107, 108, 112, 114, 115, 119, 122, 123, 127, 129, 132, 136-138,142, 145, 146, 151, 154, 155, 159
Prabhākara, 3, 12, 63, 66, 70, 71, 109, 148, 151- 153
Practical utility of Upamāna, 67, 75, 82, 109, 147, 149, 152, 154, 156
Prakaraṇapañcika, 3n, 29n, 44n, 66n, 94n
Pramā 2-6, 11, 137
parmā, 2, 6, 7, 9-14,25, 31, 37, 40, 59-62, 120, 123, 129, 135, 149
Pramāṇacandrikā,137
Pramāṇamīmāṁsā34n, 130n, 131, 131n
Pramāṇanayatattvāloka,5n
Pramāṇapaddhati, 89n, 90, 137, 139
Pramāṇaprakaraṇa, 32n, 39n, 45, 79, 89, 137, 137n, 138n,139, 141, 141n
Pramāṇasamplava, 62
Pramāṇavārttika,3n, 6n
Prameyakamalamārtaṇḍa, 58n, 77n, 78n, 129n, 130, 131n,
Praśastapāda, 5, 43, 51, 114

Praśastapādabhāṣya, 5n, 35n, 43n, 51n,114n
Prasthānaratnākara, 4n, 32n, 33n, 39n-41n,79n,142, 142n- 144n
Pratibhā,12
pratyabhijñā 39,129
presumption, 12, 36, 78, 87, 106 -108, 112, 117, 155, 157
Probandum, 46, 89-91, 93, 94,127,139
Probans, 8, 14, 44-48, 50, 55,89-91, 93, 94, 100, 107, 109, 127, 139, 150, 156
purpose of Upamāna,23, 32, 40, 42
Puruṣottama, 39-41, 79, 142, 155,159
Pūrvamīmāṁsā, 3,4,6,12,63, 109,110,147, 148, 152, 158, 159,
Pūrvamīmāṁsakas, 63, 147, 151, 1d57
Rāghavendratīrtha, 45, 45n, 141, 141n
Rāmarudri, 50n
relity, 2
recognition, 27, 31, 39, 58, 59, 129, 130, 134, 135, 155, 158, 159
remembrance, 6, 25-27, 29, 31, 36, 40, 57, 59, 60, 61, 64-67, 75-78, 80, 81, 84-87, 93, 94, 101, 102, 105, 106, 108, 113, 116- 108, 121, 123, 125, 127, 135, 139, 142, 151, 152, 154-157, 159
Śabra, 63, 64, 66, 152
Śābarabhāṣya, 63n
Sādharmya, 19, 149
sādharmyopamāna, 21, 22, 45, 140, 146, 159
sādhya, 88
Śālikanātha, 29, 41, 66, 67, 70, 159
sāmānyatodṛṣṭānumāna, 64
sambhava, 12
Śaṁkaramiśra, 36, 43, 44, 116, 150
Sāṁkhyas, 5-7, 12, 34, 75, 119, 122, 132, 154, 158, 159
Sāṁkhyancandrikā, 38-9, 39n, 44, 44n, 22, 122n, 158
Sāṁkhyakārika, 52n,119, 119n, 122n
Sāṁkhyatattvakaumudā, 5n, 11n, 35n, 38n, 44n, 52n, 75, 78, 78n,79n,121n, 122n
Śāntarakṣita, 33, 46, 59, 77, 78, 80, 97, 123, 155, 158
Śāśtradīpikā, 5n, 7n, 65n,
savikalpa, 81, 113
sense-object contact, 11, 26, 28, 40, 41, 100, 102, 116, 157
Siddhasena, 6
similarity, 13, 15, 17, 18, 21, 22, 25-27, 29, 31, 32, 34, 35, 38-40, 42, 43, 46-48, 57, 60, 61, 65, 66, 68-74, 76, 77, 79-83, 85-92, 94, 95, 97, 99, 101-107, 109, 110, 113, 115, 119, 121, 128, 131, 132, 134, 138-140, 144, 145-147, 148, 151, 152, 155-157
Ślokavārittika, 25, 26n-28n, 39n, 40n, 54n,64,74n, 65n, 67n-70n, 80n, 85n, 90, 91n, 92, 93n
smaraṇ, 129
smṛti, 6, 108, 113, 135, 158
Śrīdhara, 5, 35, 38, 40, 43, 44, 51, 75, 78, 80, 84, 87, 101, 102, 114, 115, 117, 118, 155, 157, 159

Śrīnivāsadāsa, 31, 39, 40, 53, 132, 135, 158
Śrīnivāsatīrtha, 45n, 137,
Śrutyantakalpavalli, 4n,
Śuddhādvaita, 4, 12, 32, 78, 142, 155
svalakṣaṇa, 159
syllogism, 30, 44, 48, 75, 88, 90, 100, 101, 139, 150, 155
tarka, 129
Tarkabhāṣā(Bauddha), 34n, 74n, 125n, 128n, 130n, 131n
Tarkasaṁgraha, 3n
Tārkikarakṣā, 22n, 23n, 90
Tattvasaṁgraha, 3n, 33n, 34n, 39n, 59, 60n, 76, 77n, 78n, 82, 83n, 123n-128n
Udayana, 38, 52, 48, 49, 51, 53, 56-58, 72, 75, 87, 114, 116, 134, 150, 154, 155, 159
Uddyotakara, 14, 15, 17-19, 21, 24, 38, 39, 41, 50-55, 115, 122,123, 148-150
Umāsvāti, 129
Upamānābhāsa, 19
upamiti, 15-17, 19, 64,65, 91, 98,99, 129
Uttaramīmāṁsā, 4, 12, 29, 30, 32, 33, 78, 98, 109, 132, 137, 142, 145, 147, 155, 157, 159
Vācaspatimiśra, 5,11, 14, 18, 21, 35, 38, 44, 47, 52, 54, 61, 78, 79, 121,123, 148-150,155, 158
Vādidevasūri, 5
Vaidharmyopamāna, 19, 21, 22, 140, 146, 149
Vaiśeṣikas, 5, 6, 12, 35, 43, 57, 70, 87, 114, 153, 158, 159
Vaiśeṣikasūtra, 114
Vaiśeṣikasūtropaskāra, 36n, 43, 44n, 116n
Varadarāja, 90
Vātsyāyana, 2, 14-16, 16n, 17, 21, 23, 25, 37, 38, 47, 50, 53, 55, 121, 122, 148, 149. 150
Vedāntadeśika, 30, 39, 83, 88, 133, 158
Vedāntaparibhāṣā, 4n, 98, 99n, 101n
Vedāntins, 105, 158
Veṅkaṭanātaha, 52, 53, 78, 80, 132, 155, 159
verbal testimony, 8, 12, 14, 18, 28, 30-39, 50-52 54-57, 59-63, 79, 89, 107, 111, 112, 114, 115, 119, 120, 122, 123, 129, 132, 135-138, 142, 145, 146, 150, 151, 155, 158, 159
vidyā, 5
Vijñānabhikṣu, 11, 39, 44, 122, 158
Viśiṣṭādaita, 4, 12, 30, 58, 78, 132, 137
vita, 119
vyāpti, 8, 32, 45-47, 49, 90, 139, 141, 150, 155
vyatireka, 141
vyatirekavyāpti, 50
vyatireki, 46
Yaśovijaya, 131
Yatīndramattadipikā, 4n, 31, 32n, 39n, 40n, 53n, 132, 132n, 136n,
Yoga, 7, 12
Yogasūtra, 11n
Yuktidipika, 11, 11n, 34, 35n, 38, 38n, 51n, 52, 119, 119n, 121n.